ACADIA
R E V E A L E D

MOUNT DESERT ISLAND & ACADIA NATIONAL PARK

Acknowledgements

Thanks to my mother, father, and family who always supported me. Even when they shouldn't have.

Thanks to the good people at all the museums, historical societies, and other bastions of information who graciously offered their knowledge and assistance.

Thanks to Erin for letting me put her pretty, smiling face on the cover, and Tonya who took my picture.

Thanks to Bryan Seabury, Taylor Hamra, Matt Shevlin, Grant Kernan and Josia Lamberto-Egan who kept me sane during the layout of this book.

Thanks to S.B. Livermoore, who will never be forgotten.

ISBN 0-9678904-9-7
Library of Congress Catalog Card Number 00-090752

Printing History
1st edition - 2000

All photographs, illustrations, and text by Jay Kaiser unless stated otherwise.
Edited by noted English professor Pauline Kaiser.

Although every attempt has been made to ensure the accuracy of information within this guide, the author and publisher do not assume and disclaim any liability to any party for any loss or damage caused by errors or omissions. Information has been obtained from sources believed to be reliable, but its accuracy and completeness are not guaranteed.

Also note: Some activities mentioned and portrayed within this book are inherently danger-ous. Due to the unpredictability of nature and the limits of certain individuals, the author does not assume any responsibility for injuries, physical or mental, that may be incurred while engaging in activities pictured or mentioned in this guide. By purchasing this book you acknowledge and accept this disclaimer.

Send comments or suggestions to

Papyrus Travel Guides
PO Box 1134
Northeast Harbor ME 04662

Photo on preceding page and back cover photo of peregrine falcons courtesy National Park Service

from the
author

For as long as I can remember, I have spent at least part of every summer on Mount Desert Island. Growing up in a nearby town, my family would always make a point to take time out and enjoy the only national park in New England. From wading in tidepools as a toddler, to my first hike at age six, to college summers working in Bar Harbor, the area has always held a special fascination for me.

The idea for this book came about a few summers back after bumping into an old friend from school in Bar Harbor. She was in town for a few days with her boyfriend, here to see the island they'd heard such good things about. Almost rhetorically I asked her - Lilah is her name - what she thought of Mount Desert. "It's so tacky," Lilah told me, "all trinket stores and tourist traps." I had seen this problem before, and I knew exactly what I needed to do. Going back to her place, we sat down in front of a giant map of Mount Desert, and I proceeded to mark down points of interest that should not be missed. Before I left, we agreed to meet up again to see how things turned out. By the end of her visit Lilah was ecstatic. Her take on the island had done an about face. All it took was someone to point her in the right direction.

I conceived this book as a total resource for any visitor to Mount Desert Island. Whatever you'd like to accomplish, *Acadia Revealed* will tell you what you need to know to do it right. Go for a sail on a four-masted schooner, take a walk past the Rockefeller boathouse, sample the world-renowned shellfish - make the most of your time here and find out for yourself what makes Mount Desert one of the most intriguing islands in the world.

don't

TOP ATTRACTIONS ON MOUNT DESERT ISLAND
miss out

151 SOMESVILLE
One of the prettiest towns in Maine.

43 PARK LOOP ROAD
Drive through the heart of Acadia National Park.

73 CARRIAGE ROADS
Hike, bike, or go horse back riding on the 57-mile network of Rockefeller Carriage Roads.

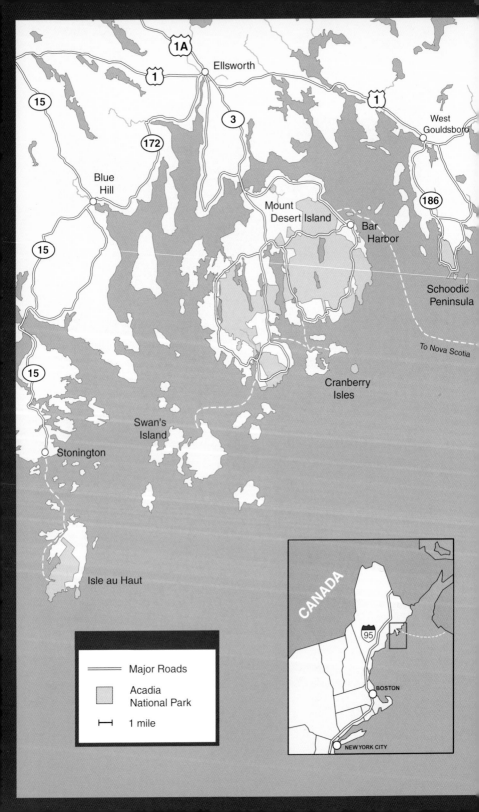

Introduction

HALFWAY UP THE COAST of Maine lies the island of Mount Desert. At 107.77 square miles, it is the third largest island off the coast of the continental United States - next to Long Island and Martha's Vineyard. Glacially carved mountains tower over the rocky shore, laying claim to the highest points on the Atlantic seaboard north of Rio de Janeiro. The wide range of temperate zones makes Mount Desert home to over 350 species of plant and animal life. All this combines to produce one of the most stunning and unique landscapes in America.

Although first mapped by Samuel Champlain in 1604, the island's remote location allowed it to slip under the national radar until it was discovered by landscape artists in the 19th century. Their paintings ushered in a tourist boom that continues to this day. Considered a close rival to Newport, Rhode Island, at the turn of the century, Mount Desert has since carved out its niche as a popular summer getaway where visitors come to enjoy the island's multitude of outdoor activities.

Over a third of the island has been permanently preserved as Acadia National Park. Acadia was the first national park established east of the Mississippi and the first created entirely out of privately donated land, a feat made possible by the island's large number of wealthy summer residents. Over 130 miles of hiking trails wrap and wind their way over and around the park's seventeen mountain peaks, sharing the land with an additional 57-mile network of horse drawn Carriage Roads personally commissioned by John D. Rockefeller, Jr.

Outside the boundaries of Acadia National Park lie the island's six major villages. Although Bar Harbor serves as the unofficial headquarters of Mount Desert, the less visited villages all contain activities, landmarks, and picture perfect coastal scenery worthy of attention. Several smaller offshore islands lie within a short boat ride of Mount Desert, ready to be explored by anyone willing to catch the next ferry across.

Finally, the outdoor activities available on Mount Desert Island could easily keep you occupied for an entire summer. In addition to hiking and biking, there's rock climbing, coastal kayaking, canoeing, and sailing all within easy reach. There's plenty to do, so get out there and enjoy the fresh air!

Courtesy National Park Service

The original Island Explorer

Getting Around Mount Desert Island

By Car
Although parking can get tight at popular destinations during July and August, this is probably the most convenient way to get around the island. There are only a handful of major roads on Mount Desert, and they are very easy to follow.

By Bike
If you're an avid biker, chances are you can easily make it around the entire island in one day. However, if your closet isn't full of spandex but you still like the idea of exploring Mount Desert via bicycle, you should stick to the eastern half of the island, where the network of gravel Carriage Roads is located. Well suited for bicycle use, these roads can take you to and from Bar Harbor, Seal Harbor, and Northeast Harbor without having to worry about the passing automobiles you'd encounter on the major roads.

By the Island Explorer Buses
These free shuttles run on regular schedules throughout the day and stop at nearly every destination listed in this book. Although less flexible than driving your own car, this is a simple and easy way to get around the island. You can pick up a free Island Explorer map that contains routes and schedules at the Hulls Cove Park Visitor Center, the Thompson Island Information Center located next to the Trenton Bridge, or various information centers in towns around the island.

History 11

Acadia National Park 33

Towns 125

history

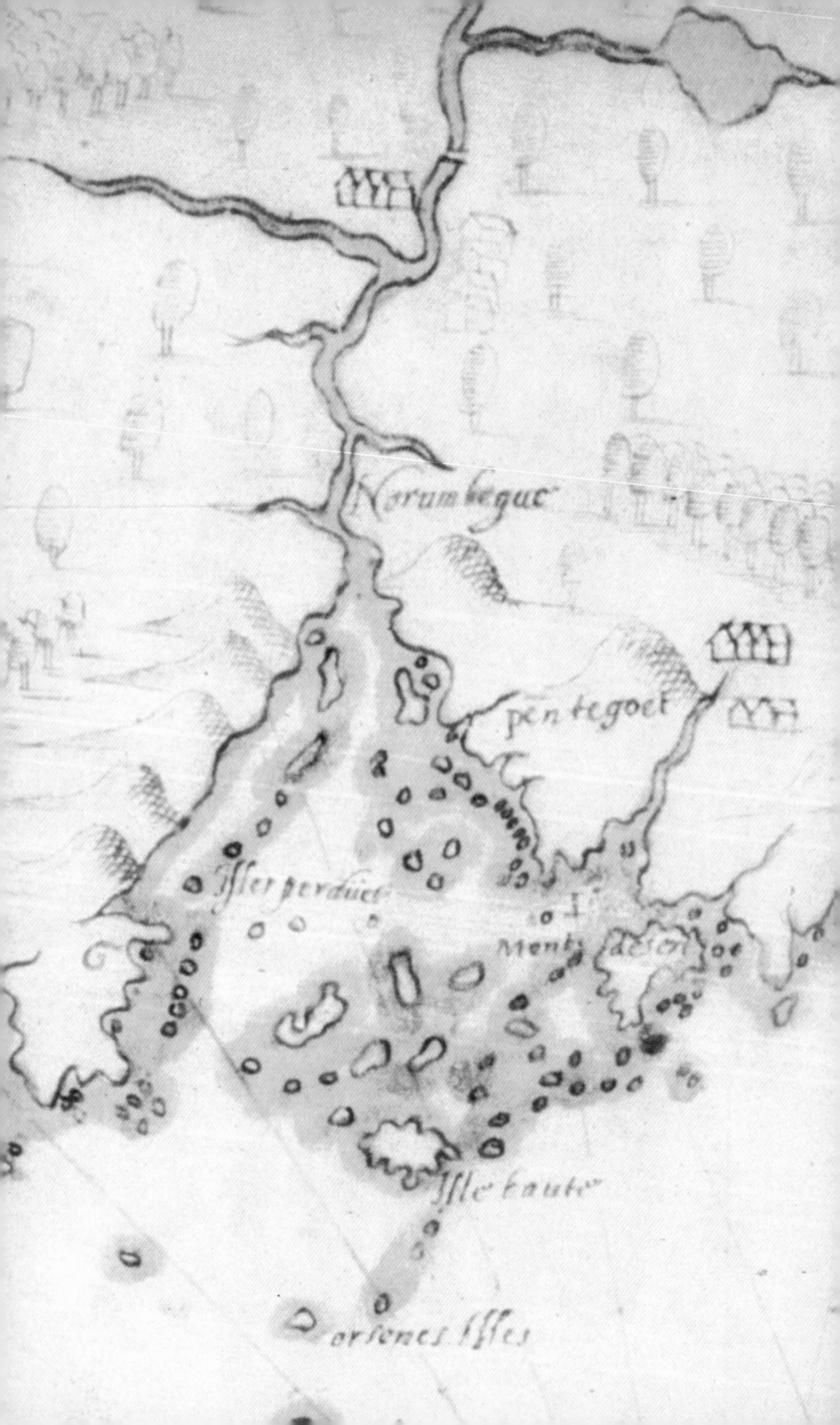

Norumbegue

pentegoet

Isle perdue

Mont deser

Isle haute

Dortenes Isles

THE COAST OF MAINE is believed to have formed roughly 550 million years ago on an ancient continent called Avalonia. Very little is known about Avalonia other than the fact that it existed somewhere east of North America and was separated from Eurasia by a body of water known as the Iapetus Ocean. At that time volcanic ash and other sediments accumulated in the waters off Avalonia, which were ultimately compressed into layers of metamorphic rock. One hundred and fifty million years later, the process was repeated, creating a second rock base. A series of lava flows formed yet another layer of rock. These three formations served as the bedrock of Avalonia.

The theory of plate tectonics states that the crust of the earth is composed of a series of rigid plates that float on the molten mantle. These plates, which make up the continents, are constantly in motion and occasionally bump into one another. Geologists believe this is exactly what happened to North America, Avalonia, and Eurasia roughly 380 million years ago. This collision not only fused the continents together but generated enough heat to melt several pockets of rock miles below the earth's surface. The resulting magma then rose toward the surface and found its way into cracks in the bedrock. When the magma cooled, it formed the large deposits of granite that would ultimately compose the core of Mount Desert. At the time, however, these deposits were still buried under thick layers of bedrock. It was not until glaciers scoured the region millions of years later that this granite would be revealed. In the meantime, as the Earth's plates continued to rearrange themselves, Eurasia broke away from North

The first known map of coastal Maine. Samuel Champlain, 1607.
Courtesy Library of Congress

America, leaving a small portion of Avalonia behind to become the stretch of coastline extending from Massachusetts to Maritime Canada.

For the next 300 million years no major changes occured in the region's topography. Then, two million years ago the worldwide climate cooled by roughly 10 degrees Fahrenheit. This drop in temperature led to

AT ITS MAXIMUM EXTENT, THE WISCONSIN GLACIATION COVERED MOST OF NEW ENGLAND AND BURIED MOUNT DESERT UNDER A SHEET OF ICE NEARLY A MILE THICK.

an accumulation of snow that ultimately formed enormous continental glaciers. As the glaciers moved from their inland formations out to sea, they scoured the landscape, drastically altering the appearance of the continents. Evidence suggests that over the past million years there have been at least nine periods in which glaciers have advanced and retreated over the northern sections of the globe. Glacial activity tends to follow consistent cycles in which glacial periods last roughly 80,000 years with warm interglacial epochs of between 15,000 to 20,000 years. We are currently 15,000 years into the most recent interglacial cycle.

The last glacial period is referred to as the Wisconsin glaciation, named after the state in which its effects are most prominent. At its maximum extent, the Wisconsin glaciation covered every mountain peak in New

Making Mountains

Glaciers cause erosion in two ways. The first, called *abrasion*, occurs when rock fragments carried at the base of the glacier scrape against the land. Picture a giant sheet of sandpaper scratching over the earth's surface. The second method, called *plucking*, occurs when built-up pressure melts the ice at the base of a glacier and the water seeps into bedrock cracks. When the water refreezes, it expands, producing enough pressure to force the rock apart. As the glacier carries away the separated rock, sheer cliffs are often left behind.

England, reached as far south as Long Island, and buried Mount Desert Island under a sheet of ice nearly a mile thick. As the glacier advanced over the island, it gouged out large U-shaped valleys, eroding much of the original bedrock and exposing the underlying granite that you see today. When temperatures rose 13,000 years ago, the Wisconsin glaciation started to retreat. Once gone, the land surface left behind underwent a process known as rebound. The tremendous weight of glaciers significantly compresses the land they cover - on Mount Desert the land was pushed down roughly 1,000 feet. When the glacier retreated the ground slowly began to rise to its original levels. The shape of Mount Desert as we know it today emerged roughly 8,000 years ago. When temperatures rose the glacier melted, flooding nearly 300 miles of coastline before stopping at their current levels. The big melt also flooded inland valleys carved out by the glacier, creating such freshwater bodies as Jordan Pond and Eagle Lake on Mount Desert.

Aerial view of Bar Harbor
From left, Champlain, Dorr, and Cadillac Mountain

The Island's First Tourists

NATIVE AMERICANS FIRST SETTLED Mount Desert Island around 1000 B.C. The Wabanaki people were hunters and gatherers, seasonally migrating from inland settlements to the coast to take advantage of Mount Desert's natural bounty. They referred to the island as "Pemetic," an Algonquin word that has been translated to mean "range of mountains" or "sloping land."

Early European records stated the Wabanaki spent their summers on the coast, returning inland during the harsh winters. However, recent evidence suggests this pattern of migration was only adopted in response to the lucrative fur trade. Prior to European contact, it is believed that the Wabanaki spent their summers at an inland settlement near present day Bangor, visiting Mount Desert only in the winter months. Since the ocean tends to have a winter warming effect along coastal areas, this theory makes practical sense.

An ancient Wabanaki settlement unearthed at Fernald Point, just north of Southwest Harbor, provides a small glimpse into their daily lives. Archaeologists believe that between 25 and 50 people lived at the Fernald Point Settlement at any given time. Soft-shelled clams and blue mussels

People of the Dawn

The following creation myth tells of how the deity Gluskap created the Wabanaki people: In the beginning there was just the sea and the forest - no people and no animals. Then Gluskap came. He possessed great magic. Out of the rocks he made the Mihkomuwehsisok, fairies who dwelt among the rocks and made wonderful music on the flute. Next Gluskap made the people. With his bow he shot arrows into the trunks of the ash trees. Out of the trees stepped men and women. They were strong and graceful people with light brown skin and shining black hair. Gluskap called them Wabanaki, "people of the dawn."

were gathered and cooked by steaming them on rock hearths. The Wabanaki also dined on deer, bear, stripped bass and haddock. Lobsters seem to have been avoided as a source of food, although sea urchins, seals, and porpoises were eaten.

Like many Native Americans, the Wabanaki soon fell victim to previously unknown European diseases. Smallpox and the bubonic plague wiped out an estimated seventy-five percent of the region's native population, and those that did survive found their ancient way of life forever changed.

A Fabled City of Gold

ALTHOUGH MANY HISTORIANS BELIEVE Norsemen may have been the first Europeans to discover the region, the first written account comes from Giovanni De Verrazano in 1524. A Florentine sailing under the French crown, Verrazano claimed to have interacted with a native people who "dress in skins of bears, wolves, seals, and other animals." He named the region "L'Acadie," based on a Wabanaki word for "land" that had favorable connotations.

Following Verrazano's discovery, rumors of a fabled city of gold began to spread in European circles. This city, referred to as Norumbega, quickly captured the imagination of many an adventurous explorer. Although its exact location was unknown, Norumbega was believed to exist somewhere along the Penobscot River, which empties into the Atlantic just south of Mount Desert.

It was with Norumbega in mind that Pierre du Gua, Sieur de Monts, a French royalist, set sail from France, reaching North America in 1604. Recently given the title Lieutenant General of New France by Henry IV, de Monts sailed with an eclectic crew that includ-

SAMVEL CHAMPLAIN

ed nobles, exiled prisoners, priests, ministers, and young volunteers. Landing at the mouth of the St. Croix River, de Monts quickly established a settlement but sent his pilot and cartographer, Samuel de Champlain, off to further explore the region.

Born the son of a captain in the Royal Navy, Champlain had previously traveled to Panama, Mexico, and the West Indies. On September 5, 1604, Champlain spotted the bald peaks of Mount Desert. He noted in his log:

> The island is very high and notched in places, so that there is the appearance to one at sea, as of seven or eight mountains extending along near each other. The summit of most of them is destitute of trees, as there are only rocks on them. The slopes are covered with pines, firs, and birches. I named it *L'isle des Monts-Deserts*.

Champlain is credited with being the first to map the region, which opened up the area to countless other explorers.

Although the fabled city of Norumbega was never found, it inspired much of the early exploration of the region. Legend had it that the cliffs surrounding the city contained so much silver their shine could be seen for miles. Men wore chest plates made of pure gold while women draped themselves in pearl-studded jewelry. A giant wall supposedly surrounded the golden city, protecting its otherwise defenseless inhabitants. Modern scholars have suggested that the legend of Norumbega may have originated as a mistranslation of the word "wealth" between Europeans and Native Americans. While natives viewed wealth in terms of natural resources like plant and animal life, Europeans were quick to interpret the word as reference to precious metals.

The French Jesuit Massacre

HAVING FAILED TO FIND Norumbega, de Mont's luck took a further turn for the worse when King Henry IV was assassinated and his successor, Louis XIII, revoked de Mont's land charter to the area. The lands of New France were given instead to Antoinette de Pons, Marquise de Guercheville, a French noblewoman who proposed a Jesuit mission in the area. Aboard the sailing vessel *Jonas* a crew of roughly 70 settlers set sail from Honfleur, France, on March 12, 1613. Attempting to land near the mouth of the Penobscot (dreams of finding Norumbega were not so quickly forgotten), the Jesuits found themselves surrounded by a terrible fog that forced them to anchor off Mount Desert. Soon after making their way onto shore, they were approached by a group of natives who informed them that their leader, Sagamore Asticou, was mortally ill and needed their immediate attention. Making their way to Manchester Point, in what is now Northeast Harbor, they found Asticou in a less than terminal condition. Some historians have speculated that Asticou actually faked sickness to draw the foreigners near and convince them to form a settlement, perhaps to benefit from the booming European fur trade. Regardless of the Sagamore's true condition, the Jesuits did decide to stay. Asticou was baptized and the settlers named their mission Saint Sauveur, "Holy Savior," in honor of their safe deliverance.

Within weeks of the French arrival, King James I of England claimed Mount Desert and the surrounding lands as his own. In order to establish his dominance, the King ordered Samuel Argall of Jamestown, Virginia, to eliminate all French settlements along the coast. Sailing just south of Mount Desert, Argall happened upon a group of Wabanaki fishing near the offshore islands. Assuming that the Europeans were friends of the Jesuits, the Wabanaki accidentally tipped them off to the defenseless settlement. By the time they realized their error, it was too late. Argall's ship, the *Treasurer*, sailed into Somes Sound ready to attack.

Although the Jesuits managed to put up a weak fight, the British easily overpowered them and laid their settlement to waste. Of the prisoners taken, a small group was allowed to flee to Nova Scotia in an open boat, while the rest were taken to Jamestown. A few weeks prior to the attack, Father Pierre Biard, the Jesuits' spiritual leader had written of the Wabanaki: "They consider themselves better than the French; 'For,' they say, 'you are always fighting and quarreling among yourselves; we live peaceably. You are envious and are all the time slandering each other; you are thieves and deceivers; you are covetous, and are neither generous nor kind; as for us, if we have a morsel of bread we share it with our neighbor, they are saying these and like things continually...'"

150 Years of Solitude

FROM 1613 TO 1760, while the British and French fought over ownership of the region, Mount Desert became a virtual no man's land. No further settlements were attempted and the island's mountainous landscape was used only as a navigational tool.

But eighty-four years after the French Jesuit settlement fell to the hands of the British, a young French military officer was granted 100,000 acres along the coast of Maine that included Mount Desert. Undaunted by the violent land disputes in the region and hoping to raise his limited social status, the ambitious Antoine Laumet sailed to the New World. Upon landing at Mount Desert, Laumet proceeded to change his name to the noble sounding, yet completely fabricated, Antoine de La Mothe, Sieur de Cadillac, based on a small village in France. But Mount Desert offered little

AN **IRRITABLE BRAWLER**, YET HIGHLY EDUCATED AND AN **ELOQUENT WRITER**, SOME HAVE PROPOSED THAT CADILLAC PROVIDED THE INSPIRATION FOR **CYRANO DE BERGERAC**.

in the way of social mobility and he headed west after only one summer. Ultimately Cadillac became a wealthy fur trader and the founder of Detroit, Michigan. Along with his invented name, Cadillac fabricated a coat of arms that can be seen today gracing the hood ornaments of millions of Cadillac automobiles.

When the British claimed victory in the French and Indian War, the Treaty of Paris put an end to disputed land claims in the region. Mount Desert's lonely exile came to an end in 1762, when Abraham Somes and James Richardson brought their families to the island and established the first permanent settlement at what is now Somesville. Mount Desert's vast supply of natural resources made it extremely attractive to ambitious settlers, and after several decades the island was growing by leaps and bounds. At first development occurred on the western side of Mount Desert, due to its close proximity to coastal shipping routes. Soon settlement spread throughout the island, and in 1796 the town of Eden (present-day Bar Harbor) was incorporated. Fishing, shipbuilding, lumbering, and farming were the area's primary occupations, and for the most part islanders lived quiet, peaceful, and productive lives.

Though the resident population of Mount Desert Island continued to grow through the mid 1800s, access to the island was still quite difficult. Traveling to the island was a multi-day affair that involved riding a train to Portland, a steamboat to Castine, and finally a sailing schooner to Mount Desert. Although the island was on the map, it was hardly in the public conscience. All that would change with the arrival of the painter Thomas Cole.

The Painted Fjord

IN 1844 AMERICAN CITIES FACED immense growing pains. Overpopulation and the effects of the industrial revolution had transformed previously habitable cities such as Boston, New York, and Philadelphia into filthy, crowded urban nightmares. A lack of modern sanitation only added to the problem. It is no coincidence that at the same time the art world experienced an overwhelming demand for landscape paintings.

Searching for new scenery to stimulate this exploding market, landscape painter Thomas Cole arrived at Mount Desert late in the summer of 1844. Accompanied by his artist friend Henry Pratt, the two spent their time sketching dramatic scenes of Sand Beach, Otter Cliffs, and Frenchman's Bay, which were later completed as paintings in their studios. When Cole's finished work was first exhibited in New York the following sum-

Salisbury Cove Church

mer, it opened to mixed, but predominately negative, reviews. One critic from *The Broadway Journal* went so far as to chide Cole's overactive imagination for producing a painting that depicted a "pea-green sea with ledges of red rock," noting, "the rocks are of a kind that no geologist would find a name for; the whole coast of Maine is lined with rocks nearly black in color. An artist should be something of a geologist to paint rocky scenes correctly." Apparently critics should be something of a geologist too since the silicate rich granite found on Mount Desert does, in fact, produce a red tint.

But despite their initial lack of critical success, Cole's paintings did find their way into the hearts of art buyers. And as is so often the case in American art, it was the art buyers who set the tone for future work. No one realized this more than Cole's aspiring young student Fredrick Church. Only twenty-four years old, Church was considered something of a prodigy, and after viewing Cole's work on Mount Desert, he set off to create his own paintings of the rugged landscape. Arriving in 1850, Church produced a series of paintings that were received the following year with enormous

Fredrick E. Church, *Otter Creek, Mt. Desert*, 1850
Notice the profile of a human face in the mountain and the cruciform shape in the man's shadow. Such details were typical of the Hudson School.

The Hudson River Valley School

As population and national ambition continued to grow in early 19th-century America, so too did the momentum to push the boundaries of the American frontier. Wilderness was admired not for its inherent natural beauty but rather as an obstacle to be conquered and exploited. It was in this vein that the American conservationist movement was born.

Leading the charge to protect the unique American landscape were the painters of the Hudson River Valley School of art. In 1847 Thomas Cole, a prominent member of the movement, summed up the Hudson School's philosophy, stating, "Yankee enterprise has little sympathy with the picturesque, and it behooves our artists to rescue from its grasp the little that is left before it is for ever too late." By portraying the American wilderness as an extension of God and a symbol of national pride, the Hudson School hoped to dispel the notion of land as an obstacle. It worked. In addition to Mount Desert, paintings of the Catskill Mountains and Niagara Falls were runaway hits and permanently established these areas as major tourist destinations.

So how did they do it? Obviously the breathtaking scenery sparked the interest of many a would-be tourist, but far more revealing are the subtle visual techniques that these artists employed. One of the most popular was to hide human faces in the contours of the rocks that they painted. Not only did this trick turn picture viewing into a kind of game; but by infusing anthropomorphic details into their works, the artists established a direct link between man and nature. Furthermore, since these landforms were considered the work of a divine Creator, the paintings also presented an intimate relationship between God and man. This connection to God was further highlighted through the frequent use of cruciform shapes.

The underlying themes explored in these paintings ultimately helped change the national perception of American wilderness. Natural settings were presented not as an open threat to man, but rather as a familiar and inspiring destination. Suddenly wilderness seemed much less an obstacle to progress and more a source of personal and spiritual enlightenment.

The ideas presented here are explored in depth in "Inventing Acadia", by Farnsworth Art Museum curator Pamela Belanger. ISBN 0-918749-09-3

critical success. Critics, patrons, and the art-going public alike all raved over his dramatic sea and sky-scapes. Both Church and the island of Mount Desert were suddenly catapulted to the forefront of the American Landscape movement.

The Rusticators

THE INTENSE DEMAND FOR Mount Desert landscapes, and Church's work in particular, led to further island excursions. Other artists, eager to cash in on the boom, also made the northern pilgrimage to capture the unspoiled wilderness scenes. The popularity of their paintings suddenly transformed the island into a haven for artists, explorers, and intellectuals seeking to enhance their relationship with an increasingly diminished natural world.

In 1855 Church arrived at Mount Desert accompanied by a group of 26 urbanites eager to witness the island first-hand. The mixed crew included artists, writers, lawyers, businessmen, and their female acquaintances. For an entire summer this early tourist party lived in meager accommodations and spent the great majority of their time hiking, fishing, picnick-

NOW, MOST OF THE VISITORS TO MOUNT DESERT, EVEN THE PROSAIC FOLK, GO PREPARED TO ENJOY THE PICTURESQUE, THE BEAUTIFUL, THE SUBLIME."
-OLIVER B. BUNCE, 1872

ing, and enjoying the healthful aspects of outdoor life. Nights were filled with endless piano playing and Church's "perfectly inexhaustible" capacity for entertainment. Although artists were present, the trip was first and foremost a social expedition. What little drawing was done tended to consist of humorous sketches mocking one another.

What seems like an infinitely satisfying summer vacation actually set the tone for the next wave of visitors on Mount Desert Island. Later named "Rusticators" these early tourists made the long journey north seeking to saturate themselves in the American wilderness experience. Not content simply to visit Mount Desert vicariously through the paintings they had seen in exhibitions, they had to witness the island's beauty first-hand. Rusticators required no fancy accommodations, often renting out empty attic space from local inhabitants and paying for a spot at the family's dinner table. Islanders, eager for extra cash, were more than happy to accommodate the easy-to-please adventurers, creating a wonderfully symbiotic relationship. Rusticators also socialized with the local Wabanakis who taught them how to fish and hunt. In 1872 noted travel writer Oliver B. Bunce summed up the rusticators' lifestyle when he wrote, "Now, most of the visitors to Mount Desert, even the prosaic folk, go prepared to enjoy the picturesque, the beautiful, the sublime."

The Cottagers

As STORIES, ARTWORK, AND MAGAZINE ARTICLES pertaining to Mount Desert found their way to a national audience, interest in the island reached new highs. However, the role of the island as a summer destination was limited by the physical challenge of actually getting there. Few potential tourists had the time, money, or patience required to make the journey. It wasn't until 1868 that direct steamboat service was provided from Boston to Mount Desert. A steamer route not only drastically cut the time it took to

Courtesy Bar Harbor Historical Society

1890s Garden party at the Bar Harbor Kebo Club

reach the island but also dramatically increased the reliability of the voyage. But the possibility of a vacation was still limited to citizens with large amounts of both time and money on their hands; the same kind of citizens who found themselves predisposed to buying expensive artwork. Although only slightly conceived as such, the paintings of Church and Cole proved to be one of the most successful tourist marketing campaigns ever undertaken.

In 1872 an article in *Harper's* featured Bar Harbor as the nation's premier summer destination, and soon anyone who was anyone had penciled in a visit to Mount Desert. The flood of visitors was a boon to the local economy. Ambitious residents began building modest hotels to accommodate the wealthy vacationers, and between 1868 and 1882 at least one hotel was built or thoroughly expanded each year. The largest, the six-story Rodick House, contained over four hundred rooms, was capable of seating over a thousand guests for dinner, and claimed to be the largest hotel in New England. At the height of its popularity rooms at the Rodick House had to be reserved two years in advance. 1882 saw the arrival of such luxuries as incandescent lighting and the telephone and two years later the Bar Harbor Express railway provided service from Boston to Mount Desert in a single day. The number of summer visitors quadrupled.

The tourist explosion quickly changed the face of Bar Harbor as upscale development continued at a breakneck pace. Hotels sprouted up in Bar Harbor farmland, and quaint general stores were replaced by stores like Tiffany's and Bonwit's that showcased the latest Parisian fashions.

Bar Harbor's Most Fabulous Cottage

The most extraordinary summer cottage in Bar Harbor belonged to Edward T. Stotesbury, a poor Philadelphia boy who started working at age 12 and eventually became a senior partner at J.P. Morgan & Company. His eighty room Wingwood contained twenty-six hand carved marble fireplaces, fifty-two telephone lines, and a thirty-room servants' wing. Edward once remarked to his gardener that he would have been content with a small cottage and a supper of beans, but the legendary spending habits of his wife, Eva, ensured that that would never be the case. Those beans would have to be eaten on a plate from one of two 1,200-piece dining sets. Eva once explained to a friend that the gold fixtures in the bathrooms were very economical, for "they saved polishing, you know." Unfortunately, Wingwood was demolished in 1953 to construct the ferry terminal now used by *The Cat*.

Courtesy National Park Service

Turn of the century gathering at Sieur de Monts Spring

Seeking to distance themselves from the increasing banality of hotel life, the wealthiest visitors began building opulent mansions along the shore. So as not to appear pretentious, families such as the Vanderbilts, Rockefellers, and Astors referred to these gilded fortresses as "cottages." Soon the social epicenter had shifted from hotel lounges into exclusive private clubs.

By 1890 Bar Harbor was one of the most elite summer playgrounds in the Northeast. Among the richest of the rich, it was included as part of a spectacular seasonal tour of resorts that included Palm Springs, Florida, in the winter; Newport in the spring; Bar Harbor in the summer; and the Berkshires in the fall. Although few locals seemed to mind the excitement, complaints soon arose from less affluent summer visitors. Longtime summer resident Edwin Godkin exclaimed with disgust, "The Cottager has become to the boarder what the red [squirrel] is to the gray, a ruthless invader and exterminator .... caste has been established...the community is now divided into two classes, one of which looks down on the other." Such complaints were countered by the likes of novelist F. Marion Crawford, who in 1896 declared that Bar Harbor was home to the finest conversation found anywhere in America. Despite all this, Bar Harbor's reputation as the gilded gateway to an island of unprecedented natural beauty was firmly established, and it continued to draw visitors by the thousands.

The Summer of the *Kronprinzessin Cecile*

Courtesy Bar Harbor Historical Society

Dining Room of the *Kronprinzessin*

On July 29, 1914, the German luxury liner *Kronprinzessin Cecilie* departed New York harbor and headed home. She carried 1,216 international passengers, nearly 600 crew members, and over forty tons of German silver and gold - valued at over a quarter of a billion dollars by today's standards.

Two nights later when the vessel was just 600 miles from the English coast, Captain Charles Pollack received word that war had broken out in Europe. To make matters worse, both British and French war ships had been dispatched to overtake the *Kronprinzessin* and confiscate her treasure. Terrified guests watched helplessly as the vessel dimmed her lights, reversed her course, and quietly raced back to the then neutral United States.

Approaching the coast of North America, Captain Pollack learned that French and English ships were patrolling the waters outside every major port from Nova Scotia to the West Indies. To avoid capture he would have to find a port small enough to slip under the blockade but large enough to accommodate the 700-foot long ship. That night the captain happened to dine next to a wealthy New Yorker who summered on Mount Desert. Following the dinner the ship's course was set for Bar Harbor.

When the *Kronprinzessin* safely reached Bar Harbor, hundreds of citizens gathered at the pier to view the enormous ship that lay off the Porcupine Islands. When it became clear the German vessel was not a threat, the town enthusiastically welcomed her arrival. For the remainder of the summer the *Kronprinzessin*'s crew enjoyed the status of an illustrious guest of honor. The ship's 30-piece wind ensemble hosted weekend concerts on the Village Green and Captain Pollack quickly became the guest to have at any social function. More than one affair broke out between the ladies of Bar Harbor and the German sailors.

In November the *Kronprinzessin* was escorted to Boston under the careful watch of the U.S. Navy. A *New York Times* columnist jokingly remarked that since the Bar Harbor social season had ended, the vessel should spend the winter in Palm Beach. But the ship's moment had passed. Three years later when the United States joined the war against Germany, the ship was converted to military use and its precious cargo was confiscated.

The Momentum Shifts

BY THE TURN OF THE CENTURY, a group of concerned citizens grew alarmed at the speed of development on Mount Desert. Real estate speculation had taken hold and a modernized lumber industry was eyeing the island's vast untouched forests. Among the most concerned was former Harvard president and longtime summer visitor Charles Eliot. With the help of wealthy outdoor enthusiast George Dorr, the two organized a private group of citizens dedicated to preserving the natural beauty of Mount Desert. Through the use of private donations, the group, calling themselves the Hancock County Trustees of Public Reservations, began acquiring large tracts of land around the island. By 1916 a national monument was created, and in 1919 an act of Congress established Lafayette National Park. A decade later the name was changed to Acadia National Park.

By the time Lafayette National Park was established, Bar Harbor had reached its maximum capacity. Hotel expansion had peaked years before and further development of nearby land slowed considerably. Although Mount Desert still exercised considerable summer pull, its reputation as the nation's premiere summer destination had started to wane. The introduction of a federal income tax in 1913 and the Great Depression are often euphemistically cited as reasons for the decline, but a more likely culprit is the tremendous overexposure Bar Harbor had received. The island's meteoric rise to the top of the American social strata left many visitors weary of the pretentious attitude that followed. Once the fad had passed, Bar Harbor found itself unable to reclaim its former glory. For decades Bar Harbor found itself coasting on the legacy of the 1890s. The *coup de grace* of the Cottage Era came in 1947, when Mount Desert fell victim to the worst natural disaster ever experienced on the island.

The Great Fire of 1947

In 1947 Chuck Yeager became the first man to break the sound barrier while Humphrey Bogart, Lauren Bacall, and Gene Kelly all marched on Washington to protest the hearings of the House Un-American Activities Committee. But here in Maine people could not stop talking about the record drought that had engulfed the state. Between August and September only a quarter inch of rain had fallen. On Mount Desert plants withered and tinder-box conditions were reported throughout the island.

On October 17, a small fire broke out in the town dump north of Bar Harbor. Although firefighters managed to control the blaze, they were unable to completely put it out. When the fire started to grow, firefighters from across the state were dispatched to prevent a possible crisis from developing. Benzedrine pills were distributed to keep volunteers awake, sometimes for several consecutive days. Even the Army's Firefighting Air Corps could not fully extinguish the blaze.

Courtesy Bangor Daily News

As the fire swept across the island, it burned over 60 private estates, including those located on "Millionaire's Row", pictured here.

Courtesy National Park Service

Sand Beach parking area several years after the fire. Notice the burnt trees on Great Head to the far left.

What happened next was an unlikely combination of events that conspired to produce a raging inferno of almost inconcievable proportions. On October 23, just as the blaze was about to be declared officially out of control, gale fore winds descended on Mount Desert, whipping up flames and sending the fire on a wild tear towards Bar Harbor. Wind bursts exceeded sixty knots. At 4pm the fire covered two thousand acres. Eight hours later over 16,000 acres had burned and the fire was still moving. "It looked like two gigantic doors had opened and towering columns of roaring flames shot down upon [us]," recalled one firefighter. A sudden shift in wind direction managed to spare the downtown section of Bar Harbor, but not before sixty seven multi-million dollar estates, one hundred seventy homes, and five hotels were consumed by the blaze. The fire then raced towards Sand Beach where winds pushed the fire to the tip of Great Head, a small peninsula jutting out to sea. As winds continued to pound the island, flames leapt nearly a mile out over open ocean, forcing nearby fishermen to turn away to avoid igniting their sails.

On November 7th, three weeks after the small blaze had been reported at the town dump, the fire was declared officially out. All told, it destroyed over 17,000 acres of forest and nearly 150 million dollars worth of property by today's standards. The mansions that served as the last reminders of Bar Harbor's gilded age were gone. In the wake of the fire, hardwoods like maple, poplar, and oak replaced the evergreen spruce and fir that were destroyed.

Present Day

AS THE SCARS OF THE FIRE STARTED TO HEAL, the island rebuilt and took on a new character that has defined it to the present day. No longer regarded as a faded bastion of wealth, Mount Desert became an increasingly popular summer destination for a wide range of social classes. Coming full circle from the days of the first rusticators, the emphasis shifted away from Bar Harbor's turn of the century social registers to the multitude of natural outdoor activites found throughout the island. Park visitation has steadily climbed year after year to well over three million visitors annually. Some park authorities believe this number could double within the next two decades, but to some extent the island is still a bit of a hidden jewel. Although Acadia is the only national park in New England, Mount Desert hardly commands the same name recognition as Martha's Vineyard or Nantucket off the coast of Cape Cod. As more and more people discover the island first-hand, that may change, but it still takes enough effort for most people to get to Mount Desert to help keep down the crowds.

Although summer has traditionally been the most popular time to explore Mount Desert, more and more savy visitors are realizing that the island's crisp New England falls offer even more spectacular scenery with nearly half the crowds. Many local businesses are now remaining open well into November to accomodate the growing number of visitors. While Mount Desert sees a constant flow of visitors in the six months from May through October, the winter months transform the island into a quiet coastal community which fewer than 10,000 souls call home. But with every spring thaw comes the first wave of visitors, and between Memorial Day and Labor Day the island is bustling with activity.

acadia national park

Foot PER FOOT, Acadia is the most visited national park in America, surpassing second place Yosemite in annual visitors per square mile. Although Acadia's 40,000 acres makes it one of our smaller national parks, it lies within a day's drive of roughly 70 million American's. All told over 3.2 million people find their way to Acadia each year, making it America's eighth most visited national park.

Encompassing over a third of Mount Desert Island, Acadia passes through forest valleys, stretches over the rocky shoreline, and contains every major mountain peak on the island. Hiking trails and Carriage Roads open up the interior of the Park to anyone willing to explore it, while the Park Loop Road winds its way along the most spectacular stretch of coastline on Mount Desert before turning inland and climbing to the top of Cadillac Mountain, the island's highest peak.

The first national park established east of the Mississippi, Acadia was also the first to be created entirely out of privately donated land, a feat made possible by the island's large number of wealthy summer residents. Private donations continue to provide an important source of revenue to keep the Park in peak operating condition. In recent years multi-million dollar initiatives have been established to preserve both the Carriage Roads and hiking trails in perpetuity. Few National Parks enjoy the loyalty and support that Acadia inspires in its nearby residents.

In addition to the Park lands on Mount Desert Island, Acadia also consists of land holdings on Schoodic Peninsula to the east and Isle au Haut to the southwest. Although both lie a bit out of the way, they are much less crowded than the rest of the Park, and people who visit them rarely regret making the journey.

History

BY THE 1890S Bar Harbor had established itself as one of the nation's most elite summer colonies. Soon its ranks came to include not only those wealthy visitors who had come for the scenery, but those who simply wanted to associate themselves with the "right" social set. By the turn of the century, the emphasis had shifted from Mount Desert's natural beauty to the exclusive lifestyle that now defined Bar Harbor. Real estate speculation quickly followed, and large tracts of land were purchased along the shore for private use.

At the same time, the island's vast forest preserves found themselves potential victims to the timber industry. Although lumbering had always played a vital role in the local economy, its growth had previously been restricted by the island's inaccessible mountain terrain. Steam powered saws could only be used economically on low ground, leaving the majority of good lumber out of reach. But with the introduction of the portable, gasoline-powered saw, all that changed. Now every stretch of forest on the island was at risk of falling prey to the lucrative timber industry.

It was with these conditions in mind that some of the island's most influential summer residents grew alarmed. The wilderness beauty of Mount Desert that had attracted them in the first place was increasingly threatened and would soon, they feared, be gone. In an unprecedented move that eventually led to the creation of Acadia National Park, a private group of citizens decided to take matters into their own hands.

On August 12, 1901, the Hancock County Trustees of Public Reservations was born. Spearheaded by former Harvard president Charles Eliot and wealthy summer visitor George B. Dorr, the group's stated mission was "to acquire, by devise, gift or purchase, and to own, arrange, hold, maintain or improve for public use lands in Hancock County, Maine, which by reason of scenic beauty...may become available for such purpose." It was their aim to acquire as much property on Mount Desert as possible before real estate developers and timber executives got there first. As savy as they were civic minded, a tax exempt, public-service Charter was soon obtained from the state of Maine, and the group quickly set to work.

Although Eliot had conceived of the idea of a conservationist group, it was George Dorr who took charge. A wealthy Boston bachelor who had inherited a large textile fortune, Dorr's family had built the second summer cottage on the island. They were original rusticators, and Dorr was determined to preserve the wilderness beauty he had grown up with on the island.

The Hancock County Trustees immediately acquired two small plots of land, but it was between 1908 and 1913 that the most significant purchases were made. With the generous financial assistance of some of the island's wealthiest summer residents, the Trustees were able to acquire lands that included Cadillac Mountain, Sieur de Monts Spring, Otter Cliffs, and Eagle Lake. All told, this constituted over 5,000 acres of prime Mount Desert property.

In 1913, under pressure from a variety of sources, the Maine legislature began taking steps to revoke the Trustees' charter. Worried that it might ultimately dissolve, Dorr suggested that the Trustees donate their holdings to the national government. This was easier said than done. More government land meant more government spending, and the Trustees first had to convince the government it was worth the money.

In 1914 Dorr set off for Washington, D.C., to lobby for his cause. Well-connected in political circles, Dorr pulled strings and cashed in on favors to get what he wanted. Two years later Sieur de Monts National Monument was created. The name was based on a land title traced back to Samuel Champlain's early benefactor.

Courtesy National Park Service

George Dorr & Charles Eliot

The Father of Acadia

To say George Dorr loved Mount Desert is an understatement. The man cherished the area. Schooled for a brief time at Oxford, Dorr had traveled extensively through Europe, exploring the Scottish highlands and hiking alpine Switzerland. When he inherited his family's vast textile fortune at the turn of the century, he could have lived anywhere in the world, but he chose Mount Desert. Before organizing the Hancock County Trustees of Public Reservations, Dorr spent his time on Mount Desert immersed in outdoor activities. When he wasn't hiking or biking across the island, he was at work building new paths and outlets for such pursuits. His efforts on behalf of public recreation were the object of constant praise in the Bar Harbor community. Residents never ceased to marvel at his boundless enthusiasm for the outdoors that went so far as to include an exhilarating morning swim off the Bar Harbor pier every day until Christmas.

In 1944, at the age of 91, George Dorr died an impoverished man. He had spent his entire fortune, once valued at over 10 million dollars, purchasing additional land for Acadia National Park. Shabby clothes replaced his once expensive suits. By the end he could not even afford to buy new books. Three years before his death, Dorr donated his family homestead, Oldfarm, to Acadia National Park. Reflecting on his gift of the land where he had spent so many happy summers, he wrote, "there is nothing in my work for the Island or the Park that I look back upon with greater satisfaction or sense of permanence."

Without his constant efforts, it is doubtful that the most popular holdings of the Park would exist as we know them today.

That same year legislation was passed creating the national park system. The ball was rolling and Dorr quickly set to work to establish Sieur de Monts as a national park. Despite the government's preoccupation with the war effort, Dorr was able to gather the support he needed. On February 26, 1919, Lafayette National Park was created. The name "Lafayette" was chosen to reflect America's pro-French sentiment in the wake of World War I. Dorr happily agreed to become the Park's first superintendent.

Continuing his work to expand the Park's holdings, Dorr managed to acquire the stretch of shoreline extending from Thunder Hole to Otter Cliffs as well as Schoodic Peninsula on the mainland. The latter was donated by three sisters on the condition that the name of the park be changed from Lafayette to something less French. In 1929 President Calvin Coolidge signed an act that renamed the area Acadia National Park. Ironically, the word Acadia was first coined by a Frenchman who derived it from a local Native American term. The final addition to Acadia came when tracts of land on the southern portion of Isle au Haut were acquired in the 1940s. In 1986 Congress passed legislation that established permanent park boundaries, so as not to limit the surrounding area's economic growth.

Through the astute foresight of Charles Eliot and the tireless efforts of George Dorr, the unspoiled beauty of Mount Desert that was threatened at the turn of the century had become one of America's most cherished national parks. With the continued help of concerned citizens, this spectacular coastal landscape will remain open to the public for future generations to enjoy.

Campgrounds in Acadia National Park

Blackwoods Just north of Seal Harbor, Blackwoods is the most popular campground due to its close proximity to the Carriage Roads, hiking trails, and Park Loop Road. Open from mid June to mid September, but be aware that reservations are required. $18 per night.

Seawall Located near the Southwestern tip of Mount Desert, Seawall is open on a first come, first served basis. $18 per night.

Duck Harbor Campground Consisting of six lean-to cabins on Isle au Haut, reservations are required months in advance and competition for this pristine campground can get fierce in July and August.

For reservations call 1-800-365-2267 or visit www.reservations.nps.gov

Ranger Program on Great Head

Ranger Programs

Acadia National Park offers free, ranger-guided programs nearly every day in the spring, summer, and fall. Park rangers are consistently helpful, knowledgeable, and super-friendly people who share a passion for learning about the Park and passing on that knowledge to others. These programs are highly recommended. There are even some programs geared specifically towards children. To find out which programs will be offered during your stay, pick up a copy of the *Beaver Log*, Acadia's free reference guide that includes program schedules, tide charts, and other useful info. The *Beaver Log* is available at the Thompson Island information center, the Park Visitor Center, Blackwoods and Seawall Campgrounds, and other locations throughout the Park

Hiking and Walking Tours Ranger-led hikes last from one to three hours and usually cover no more than three miles. There are over twenty tours available that include wildlife walks, geology hikes, and nighttime stargazing at Sand Beach among others.

Boat Cruises Acadia offers three different ranger-interpreted boat cruises. Reservations are necessary and tickets are between $10-20/ person.

Amphitheater Programs One-hour evening presentations are often offered at the amphitheaters located at Seawall and Blackwoods campgrounds. Topics range from natural history lectures to photography tips.

park
loop
road

❶ Hulls Cove Visitor Center

The best place to start your drive along the Park Loop Road is at the Hulls Cove Visitor Center, located north of Bar Harbor off Route 3. To reach the main building, you'll need to climb 52 stairs - if you suffer from disabilities head up the short road at the nearby intersection to a more accessible parking lot. Inside, a free movie introducing you to the Park is shown every half-hour. An information desk is staffed with park employees ready to answer any and all questions and provide you with free park publications, including the *Access Guide* which provides information for disabled visitors. The Visitor Center also contains one of the island's most extensive selections of books on Acadia.

To start your drive on the Park Loop Road, head out of the Visitor Center the way you came in, and follow the signs. Keep in mind that the speed limit never exceeds 35 mph and it is enforced. In fact, the section of road heading out of the park visitor center is one of most popular places for speed traps. Besides, if you're driving fast, you're simply missing the point. And another thing: as you drive along the Park Loop Road, STOP FREQUENTLY AND GET OUT OF YOUR CAR! It's a spectacular drive, but the Park Loop Road's most beautiful aspects will only be revealed to you if you take the time to get out and explore.

Note: To use the milages that accompany points of interest on the Park Loop Road, set your odometer to 0 at the stop sign on your way out of the Visitor Center parking lot.

Courtesy National Park Service

Fredrick Law Olmstead, Jr., Designer of the Park Loop Road

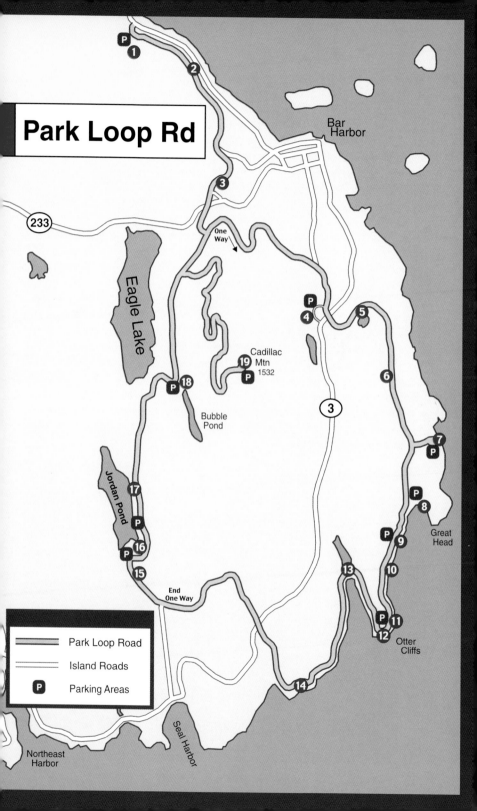

❷ Frenchman's Bay Overlook 0.5 miles

Spread out below you are the five Porcupine Islands nestled in Frenchman's Bay. From the early 1600s to the mid 1700s, the area around Mount Desert was a virtual no man's land. No permanent settlements were attempted as the British and French fought over conflicting land claims. At the height of the war, French gunboats often hid behind the Porcupine Islands waiting to attack passing English ships.

The island closest to you is Bar Island. At low tide a sand bar is exposed that connects the island to the town of Bar Harbor. Each day a three- to four-hour window allows visitors the opportunity to cross the sand bar and explore the unspoiled island. See page 131 for more details. Oddly enough, the Porcupine Islands aren't part of Bar Harbor but belong instead to the town of Gouldsboro across Frenchman's Bay.

In the late 1800s when Bar Harbor was at the pinnacle of its opulence, a summer courtship developed between Turkish Ambassador Mavroyeni Bey and a young lady from Philadelphia. Desperate to win her love, the Ambassador organized a moonlit party in her honor at the Bar Harbor Canoe Club, then located on Bar Island. Paper lanterns were hung from the trees and violinists played hidden in the woods. As wealthy guests mingled in the summer night, they were treated to a French fireworks display that included both aerial and underwater fireworks. Although the Ambassador was unable to win over the lady's love, the party is remembered as a Bar Harbor classic.

Porcupine Islands from Cadillac Mountain

3 1947 Fire Overlook 2.3 miles

The great fire of 1947 spent nearly a month tearing across the island, destroying virtually everything in its path. When it was finally extinguished, the fire had burned nearly a third of the Park's forest. Prior to the disaster, the island had been dominated by evergreens like spruce and fir, but as the forests recovered, hardwoods such as maple, poplar, and oak grew in the fire's wake. Today a mix of evergreens and hardwoods coexist on the island. Although the spruce and fir may one day reclaim their lost territory, a healthy mix is expected to exist for quite some time. From this vantage point you can trace the path of the fire, marked by the light green patches of hardwood leaves against the dark green evergreens that did not burn. This contrast becomes surreal in late fall when the brilliant yellow and orange foliage seems to re-enact the raging blaze.

Park Loop Road Junction 2.5 miles

At this point the road forks. Take a left to get on the one-way section of road that brings you to the most popular attractions. Eventually the Park Loop Road wraps around to bring you back to this point. Unless otherwise noted you can park anywhere on the right-hand side of the road along the one-way section.

Legend of the Porcupine Islands

There are no porcupines on the Porcupine Islands. The name comes from the physical shape of the islands which, with their humped shape and sharp pine trees, look like porcupines. According to a Native American legend, a giant once lived on top of Cadillac Mountain who kept five porcupines as pets. Although he specifically instructed them to never stray from the mountaintop, one day while the giant was away the five porcupines chased one another down to the island's shore. Before they could make their way back, the giant returned and realized they were gone. Unable to contain his rage, the giant let out a roar and started throwing large boulders from the mountaintop. Hearing the giant's screams, the terrified porcupines fled into the water to escape. As luck would have it, a wandering fairy happened upon the drowning porcupines and turned them into stone, forever protecting them from the giant's wrath.

④ Sieur de Monts Spring 5.7 miles

Named after Champlain's benefactor, Sieur de Monts Spring was purchased by George Dorr in 1909. Prior to the purchase, the spring had been used to bottle water commercially for sale among the summer residents. Dorr proceeded to build the octagonal cover house, based on a Florentine design, to protect the purity of the spring water. While traveling along the Bosporus strait that separates European from Asian Turkey, Dorr had visited two springs that bore the names "The Sweet Waters of Europe" and "The Sweet Waters of Asia." In a worldly homage to those springs, Dorr had "The Sweet Waters of Acadia" inscribed on a nearby stone.

It's worth stopping at Sieur de Monts Spring to explore one or all of its nature-oriented diversions. This area is also one of the best places on the island for bird watching.

Abbe Museum
Shell necklaces and bone flutes are just two of the things you'll find on display at the Abbe. This private museum is devoted to collecting, preserving, and celebrating Maine's Native American heritage. Its wide range of artifacts includes a birch bark canoe, harpoons, and the largest collection of Maine Indian baskets in the world. Inside a variety of exhibits explore the unique culture of Native Americans living along Maine's coast. Special presentations, children's programs, and workshops are offered throughout the summer. The Abbe Museum was founded in 1927 by Dr. Robert Abbe, a pioneering plastic surgeon and summer resident of Mount Desert. One day in 1922, Dr. Abbe noticed a collection of native stone tools in a Bar Harbor window display. His fascination led him to purchase the tools. When he founded the museum five years later, his collection had grown to become one of the finest of its kind. Today the Abbe is home to over 50,000 native artifacts, so many that an additional museum is currently under construction in downtown Bar Harbor. In 1999 the Abbe was selected by the American Association of Museums as one of six museums to help develop a set of national standards for museum interpretation. 207-288-3519. Spring & Fall hours: 10am - 4pm, July & August: 9am - 5pm. Small admission fee.

Sieur de Monts Spring

Wild Gardens of Acadia

In 1916 George Dorr formed the Wild Gardens of Acadia Corporation with the stated purpose of providing "sanctuaries for the plant and animal life - the flora and fauna - of the Acadia region ... a source of pleasure and a means of inspiration." After the great fire of 1947 scarred the region, a group of volunteers from the Bar Harbor Garden Club established the Wild Gardens of Acadia as we know them today. Over 500 species of plant life native to Mount Desert are showcased here. The garden is divided into twelve distinct sections to model the range of habitats present on the island, including meadows, woodlands, and sand dunes. Pick up a booklet near the entrance that contains a map, description of the garden, and list of seasonal blooms. Open 24 hours.

Nature Center

This small brown building located at the end of the parking area is worth a quick glimpse. It offers exhibits relating to Acadia's natural history and how these resources are looked after by park scientists. A park ranger is usually on duty to answer any questions you may have. Open mid-June through September, 9am - 5pm

❺ Beaver Dam Pond 6.7 miles

The small, tranquil pond on your right is host to a wide variety of animals, including ducks, otters, and most importantly beavers. The pond's water level is maintained by a beaver dam, which left unchecked would threaten both this section of the Park Loop Road and the world renowned Jackson Lab on your left. A quiet overflow pipe set in place by park rangers is used to keep the height of the pond at safe levels. If you're looking for beavers, you need to go at the right time. Eager beavers can arrive at dawn. The rest of us can look for beaver activity at dusk.

Champlain Mountain Overlook 7.3 miles

As you continue along past Beaver Damn Pond, the Park Loop Road will climb upwards for a bit and then start a gradual descent to sea level. Along the way you'll be provided with sweeping views of Frenchman's Bay to your left. From here you can see the rocky island of Egg Rock and the Egg Rock Lighthouse that guards the waters to the bay. Built in 1875, today the lighthouse is fully automated and flashes its 1000 watt, red beacon every 5 seconds. Although Frenchman's Bay contains pockets of water over 290 feet deep, it is filled with dangerous shallow ledges. Mariners use the Egg Rock Lighthouse to safely make their way to Bar Harbor.

From here the road descends to sea level

Highseas

From the Champlain Mountain overlook you will notice a large brick building perched above Frenchman's Bay to your left. This is the spectacular Highseas estate. In 1912 Princeton University Professor Rudolf Brunnow had this mansion constructed as a wedding gift for his fiance, then living in Europe. It contained 32 rooms with an 11-room guesthouse. The bricks used were specially shipped from Philadelphia. Tragically, Brunnow's fiance would never set eyes on Highseas. Her voyage home was booked on the *Titanic*, and she was among the hundreds who perished in the freezing waters of the North Atlantic.

Although Brunnow's heart did go on, locals suspected him of being a German spy during World War I. It was also rumored that a secret room lay deep within Highseas. Neither of these stories was ever confirmed.

In 1924 Highseas was sold to Mrs. Eva Van Cortland Hawkes of New York City for the princely sum of $25,000. A divorcee who never remarried, she kept mostly to herself for years. Then during World War II, Mrs. Hawkes began throwing lavish parties at Highseas for the American and British navies who were called to port. The cost of these gala events ran into the thousands. Champagne was ordered by the case and lobster Newburg was cooked in 30-gallon drums.

When the great fire of 1947 swept through this area, Highseas was spared destruction by a faithful servant who kept the mansion doused with water. Mrs. Hawkes died shortly thereafter, and the building was donated to the Jackson Laboratory.

Want to live in Highseas for a summer? Today the mansion is used as a dormitory for high school and college students participating in the Jackson Lab's annual summer program. Although favored by pre-meds, the program is open to any qualified student with a strong interest in science. Admission to the program is competitive with acceptance rates hovering around 11 percent. But if you are smart, studious, and don't mind living in opulent mansions, you can pick up an application at the Jackson Lab, located south of Bar Harbor off route 3. See page 138 for further details.

⑥ Champlain Mountain and the Precipice Trail 7.3 miles

As you continue on past Highseas, you'll see the dramatic slope of Champlain Mountain on your right. The sheer face of Champlain towers over one thousand feet above the ocean, providing some of the best views on the island.

The parking lot coming up on your right marks the beginning of the Precipice Trail, agreed by all to be the most challenging hike in Acadia. The huge boulders you see at the base of the trail were ripped off the face of the cliff when glaciers swept through the area twelve thousand years ago.

Prior to the trail's construction in 1914, most island residents believed that the cliff was far too dangerous to hike. Two climbers' lives had already been claimed, and several early path builders who attempted to find a plausible route up the face quickly abandoned their efforts. It wasn't until Rudolf Brunnow (the first owner of Highseas) tackled the task that any progress was made. Determined to construct a path for public use, Brunnow studied the cliff for months. Eventually he discovered a route that might work, but it would require the extensive use of iron ladders and rungs. Construction soon commenced.

Bar Harbor residents eagerly anticipated the completion of the path, even building a model Precipice in Bar Harbor to practice on before the trail officially opened. When finally completed, the trail lived up to every one of its lofty expectations. Its 252 steps, 183 iron rungs, and 4 ladders provided manageable, if not challenging access to the top. Although Brunnow considered several names for his masterpiece, the public had already dubbed it "The Precipice" and the name stuck. If you are in good physical shape and are not afraid of heights, you should have no problems conquering The Precipice. It is one of the most rewarding hikes on the island, and if you have the time it should not be missed. However, between May and mid-August the trail is closed to protect nesting peregrine falcons. During this time rangers will set up telescopes in the morning for public viewing of the birds, also a rewarding diversion.

See page 99 for hiking information.

The precariously precipitous Precipice

Peregrine falcons

For over a decade nesting peregrine falcons have been protected at Acadia National Park. One of the first species listed under the Endangered Species Act in 1973, peregrines faced extinction in the early '70s when their numbers reached an all time low of 39 pairs. The introduction of the pesticide DDT is blamed for the bird's decline. When DDT breaks down into DDE, the resulting chemical is passed on to organisms at the bottom of the food chain. Peregrines, located at the top of their food chain, ultimately absorbed the DDE, which caused the shells of the birds' eggs to become so fragile that they broke when the mother bird sat on them.

Although DDT was banned in 1972, the effects of the pesticide had already been felt. In an attempt to rebuild the peregrine population, young falcons were raised in captivity and then introduced into the wild. Starting in 1984 the peregrine recovery effort included sections of Acadia National Park. Each spring both The Precipice and the Jordan Cliffs hiking trails are temporarily closed to protect the nesting falcons.

Peregrines are birds of prey that prefer nesting on tall cliffs so they can dive-bomb their victims, swooping down at speeds topping 100 miles per hour. Birds that are not killed instantly upon impact have their necks broken by the peregrine's specially designed beak. The falcons are such successful strikers that they were used by British troops to kill Nazi carrier pigeons in World War II.

In August of 1999, peregrine falcons were removed from the Endangered Species list. Surprisingly, their successful recovery stems in part from the overbuilding of America's urban centers. Although peregrines were originally drawn to high cliffs, they have recently taken up residence under tall suspension bridges and on top of skyscrapers, feeding largely on pigeons and other city birds. In the late 1980s a bird released from Acadia National Park was found on top of the John Hancock Building in downtown Boston. Despite the species' overall success, populations in Maine continue to remain flat. With the continued efforts of the park staff and a little luck, hopefully that will soon change.

Peregrine falcon chicks nesting on The Precipice
Courtesy National Park Service

Sea Anemone Cave

7 Schooner Head Overlook / Sea Anemone Cave 8.6 miles

Before reaching the Park Loop Road entrance station, turn left onto a two-way road to check out the Schooner Head Overlook. The large chunk of granite jutting out into the water before you is Schooner Head. Legend has it that early mariners sometimes mistook the white markings on the ledge for the sails of a ship. According to one story, a British ship went so far as to fire upon the ledge in a snowstorm during the Revolutionary War.

But chances are you're not looking at the rock. The modern building perched atop Schooner Head is indeed a private residence. Bar Harbor town records list the owner as Dan Burt, a wealthy European financier. Mr. Burt recently completed a million-dollar addition behind the main house (before it was terribly cramped).

However, the real attraction here is the hauntingly beautiful Sea Anemone Cave. Named for the tidepools inside that contain a variety of sea life, Sea Anemone Cave has captured the imagination of tourists since the turn of the century. Thousands of years of wave action are responsible for carving out this 82-foot deep grotto. To view the cave, you will need to scamper down the rocks towards the shore. Be aware that if it has recently rained, the rocks will be quite slippery - depending on your sense of adventure, you might want to wait for a sunny day. The best route down is by the area where the paved path ends. The lower the tide, the better the vantage points. Although the cave is accessible at low tide, DO NOT GO INSIDE THE CAVE! A fragile ecological environment exists within that is threatened by human contact. If you are dying to see tidepools, sit tight. Otter Point further down the Park Loop Road has plenty of tidepools perfect for exploring.

❽ Sand Beach 10 miles

One of two natural sand beaches found on the island - the other is located in Seal Harbor - Sand Beach is one of the most popular stops along the Park Loop Road, so expect large crowds in July and August. The beach is accessible from a large granite stairway located at the far end of the parking area. Restrooms, fresh water, telephones, and changing areas are all available here. But before you get ready for that summer dip, be prepared for water temperatures that rarely exceed 55 degrees during the hottest summer months. Gentlemen should leave their Speedos at home.

The sand here is composed mostly of crushed seashells and sea urchin skeletons. Winter storms tend to pull large amounts of sand away from the beach, which is then washed back onshore in the spring. At

Sand Beach and Great Head Peninsula

times enough sand is removed to reveal the skeletal hull of the schooner *Tey*, a cargo ship transporting lumber and shingles that crashed offshore in 1911. According to personal accounts, the spring following the ship's crash, nearly every house in nearby Otter Creek sported brand new shingles. If you visit Sand Beach in late fall, look for the remains of the *Tey* near the bottom of the parking area stairs.

In 1910 JP Morgan gave Sand Beach and the surrounding lands to his daughter as a present. She then proceeded to build a summer mansion on Great Head - the peninsula to the east of the beach. When early park supporter George Dorr approached her about donating the beach to Acadia, Morgan's daughter would only agree to donate the western half of the beach, keeping the rest for her private use. JP Morgan's granddaughter donated the remaining half of the beach in 1949, two years after the great fire had destroyed the summer houses on Great Head.

Three fabulous hiking trails start near Sand Beach - The Great Head Trail, Ocean Trail, and Beehive. All are considered some of the best hikes on the island. See the Hiking section for details.

Movie Making at Sand Beach

Between 1916 and 1921, seven major motion pictures were filmed on Mount Desert. Producers loved the rugged, rocky coastline that had a natural storybook quality about it - caveman movies and mythological adventures were among the most popular to be filmed here. Although some island

Fox's 1917 *Queen of the Sea*

residents regarded the film crews as a bit of a nuisance, local resistance usually faded whenever a director announced that extras were needed. Both Sand Beach and Thurston's Lobster Pound (on the Southwest side of the island) were recently featured in John Irving's Academy Award winning film adaptation of *The Cider House Rules*.

The shipwrecked Tey *on Sand Beach*

The Ocean Trail

The stretch of shoreline extending from Sand Beach to Otter Cliffs offers some of the most dramatic coastal scenery in America. One of the best ways to soak it all in is to hike the Ocean Trail which starts next to the Sand Beach parking area and continues along the shore, passing Thunder Hole, Monument Cove, and ending at Otter Cliffs. More of a walk than a hike, the Ocean Trail is perfect for people of just about any activity level.

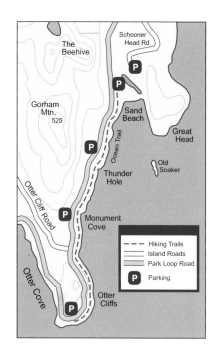

9 Thunder Hole 10.9 miles

A little past Sand Beach lies Thunder Hole, marked by a large granite sign on the left. There's a parking area on the right. If it's full, you can park in the right-hand lane of the Park Loop Road.

Thunder Hole is a geological phenomenon that when hit by the right waves at the right time produces a booming sound that can sometimes be heard for miles. As waves rush into the large crack of granite, air is compressed into a small cave located at the far end. If the pressure within the cave becomes too great, the trapped air explodes outward in a thunderous spray of surf.

Unfortunately most visitors leave Thunder Hole disappointed by the quiet sloshing sounds they've heard. The secret is to visit Thunder Hole halfway between high and low tide when the waves hit the cave just right. And if you happen to be at Acadia during or after a large storm, you should not miss the opportunity to witness nature's spectacular display at Thunder Hole.

10 Monument Cove 11.2 miles

Most people drive past Monument Cove without ever realizing it's there. This tiny cove was formed through centuries of wave action pounding against a cracked section of granite coastline. Today the cove is filled with smooth granite stones weighing nearly 40 pounds apiece. These stones started out as coarse granite chunks that were rounded out over time by the waves. The large pillar of rock on the left is the monument of Monument Cove. It was formed by a crack in the nearby granite walls that slowly eroded over time.

the monument of monument cove

Thunder Hole during an autumn storm

⑪ Otter Cliffs

One of the highest headlands on the Atlantic seaboard, Otter Cliffs towers 107 feet above the open ocean - a fact that has not been overlooked by rock climbers who can be found at Otter Cliffs nearly every day in the summer and fall. Its unique location makes it one of a handful of seaside climbs in the United States. If you're an avid climber or if you ever wanted to give it a try, Otter Cliffs is worth your while. See page 177 for details.

There are no sea otters near Otter Cliffs. In fact, there are no sea otters on the entire east coast. The name comes from nearby Otter Cove, which gets its name from nearby Otter Creek, which gets its name from nearby *river* otters that are sometimes seen there.

The area around Otter Cliffs was spared from the great fire, and as a result towering red spruce trees dominate the landscape. As the Park Loop Road approaches the top of Otter Cliffs, the right lane leads to an elevated section of road while the left lane takes a lower course. Both lanes remerge shortly thereafter - neither section is better than the other. When the Park Loop Road was first opened, it operated as a two-way road. Fredrick Law Olmstead, Jr. designed this split so that cars traveling in either direction would have equally spectacular views. From this point it's only 3,000 miles to Europe across the pond.

The green buoy bobbing just offshore marks The Spindle, a shallow rock ledge that is sometimes mistaken for a whale. Both Samuel Champlain and the French Jesuits crashed on the Spindle before the island was well mapped.

⑫ Otter Point 12.1 miles

Probably the best place in the Park to explore tidepools. There's a small parking area on the right if you plan on getting out of your car. The gently sloping granite here provides a fantastic glimpse of the inter-tidal zone, the twelve-foot vertical drop between high and low tide. As the tide falls, small pools of water filled with marine organisms are left behind. These microcosms of marine life provide a terrific glimpse of coastal animals in their natural habitat. Inside you can find starfish, sea urchins, mussels, and other interesting creatures, but be sure to leave what you find where you found it.

The inter-tidal zone is actually composed of several sub-zones which support completely different organisms depending on how much time they spend underwater throughout the day. Time spent underwater affects not only the amount of water an organism is exposed to but also the amount of air, sunlight, and predators it must contend with.

Sunrise at Otter Cliffs

Otter Cove causeway

⑬ Otter Cove   12.8 miles

After passing Otter Point, the Park Loop Road will gradually curve around Otter Cove. Many ships have crashed off Otter Point, and many have wound up here for repairs.

The picture perfect causeway that spans the cove was built in 1928. The original plan called for a solid bridge that would create a warm swimming area off the right-hand side of the road. Ultimately the plan was abandoned to preserve the peaceful setting.

⑭ Little Hunters Beach

Like Monument Cove, Little Hunters Beach is another unmarked section that most visitors overlook. The beach is notable for the small, round cobblestones that cover the shoreline and for the spectacular ocean views. This is a quiet, secluded spot, perfect for a little down time. On the left side of the road, there's a large wooden staircase that descends to the beach. During the 1800s cobblestones from Maine beaches like Little Hunters Beach were used to pave the streets of Boston, New York, and Philadelphia. Today Acadia is struggling to keep its cobblestone supply from being depleted. Although it is illegal to remove any object from the Park, these cobblestones prove to be one of the most popular keepsakes. For that reason park rangers are especially on the lookout at places like Hunters Beach. I have personally witnessed rangers scold little old ladies for attempting to remove Park stones, so don't think you'll be able to win anyone over with your charm.

⑮ Jordan Pond Gate House 18.1 miles

As you approach the Jordan Pond area of the Park, you'll notice the Jordan Pond Gate House on you right. John D. Rockefeller, Jr. had the Gate House constructed in 1932 as a checked entry point onto the Carriage Roads to ensure that automobiles stayed out.

Rockefeller believed that the structural architecture of the nation's other national parks was haphazard and disorganized. He was determined to make Acadia different. In 1929 Rockefeller sent renowned New York architect Grosvenor Atterbury on a tour of the western national parks to study their architectural faults so that the same mistakes would not be repeated on Mount Desert. Among Atterbury's most important observations:

- Buildings should not compete with the local scenery
- If an indigenous style of architecture is unavailable for reference, a suitable foreign style should be chosen.

Since no indigenous style of architecture was available on Mount Desert, Atterbury felt that French Romanesque architecture would be appropriate. This pastoral European style was a sophisticated choice that would also pay homage to the island's early French heritage.

Rockefeller and Atterbury chose a design for the Gate House based on a French hunting lodge. In accordance with his principles, Atterbury placed the structure subtly on the edge of the road where it was surrounded by forest. Today the Jordan Pond Gate House provides living quarters for lucky park personnel.

Carriage Road enthusiasts by the Jordan Pond Gatehouse

16 **Jordan Pond House** 18.2 miles

In the 1870s Melvin Tibbetts occupied a rustic farmhouse on the south shore of Jordan Pond. To earn some extra cash, the hospitable Mr. Tibbetts began offering home cooked meals to hungry hikers from Seal Harbor. As word spread, the Jordan Pond House became an increasingly popular destination. In 1895 Thomas McIntire and his wife Nellie bought the farmhouse and continued the dining tradition. Thomas added a small dining room covered in birch bark to the main farmhouse while Nellie added fresh popovers and tea to the picnic menu.

The McIntires continued to run the restaurant until 1945. By that time John D. Rockefeller, Jr. had purchased the farmhouse and donated it to the Park. Although the original Jordan Pond House burned down in 1979, the building you see before you was constructed three years later out of privately donated funds. Unlike the Gate House, the new, modern restaurant is not an example of French Romanesque architecture.

Today the tradition of popovers and tea at the Jordan Pond House continues. Behind the restaurant is an open lawn with outdoor seating that provides one of the best views on the island. Spread out before you are the crystal clear waters of Jordan Pond with the glacially formed Bubbles beyond. A popular local joke has it that the Bubbles earned their name when an early explorer first set sight on the mountains and was instantly reminded of his girlfriend, "Bubbles."

The Jordan Pond House is open from 11:30 A.M. to 8:00 P.M. Tea is served from 2:30 to 5:30. Be aware that this is one of the most popular spots on the island. In July and August you may find yourself waiting a half-hour or longer to be seated. Reservations are available and are highly recommended during peak tourist season. If you really want to look smooth in front of your family and friends, plan reservations for at least an hour before you arrive and build up an appetite by hiking the 3.5 mile Jordan Pond Shore Trail. See page 104 for details. There are also plenty of Carriage Roads in the area for hiking or biking. Public restrooms, phones, and water fountains are also located here.

If popovers and tea aren't already required by law, they should be

🟢 Bubble Rock Lookout 19.4 miles

As the Park Loop Road climbs a gentle slope, you'll be provided with a spectacular view of Jordan Pond on your left. Although not the largest body of water on Mount Desert, Jordan Pond is the deepest at 150 feet. Salmon, togue, and brook trout can all be found here. A report exists from 1870 claiming that two men once caught 500 trout in a single day of fishing at Jordan Pond. With the proper permits you can still fish here today, but expect a slightly smaller catch.

Once you reach the north end of the pond, keep your eyes out for Bubble Rock on the left. This enormous boulder, perched precariously on a cliff overlooking the Park Loop Road, is estimated to weigh between 11 and 14 tons. Remarkably, grains from the rock indicate that it was carried here from a spot nearly 20 miles away. Twelve thousand years ago a glacier swept up Bubble Rock and carried it to its present location. Although it looks as though Bubble Rock could topple over at any moment, it is actually quite secure. A short, steep hiking trail brings you directly to the boulder where you can see for yourself. See page 103 for details.

Bubble Rock

18 Bubble Pond 20.7 miles

If you're looking for a nice spot to picnic but can't deal with the crowds at the Jordan Pond House, Bubble Pond is your place. There's a small picnic table by the shore about 200 feet from the parking area. Bubble Pond was created by the gouging action of the glaciers that passed through Mount Desert. Loons are fond of Bubble Pond, so listen for their haunting call while you're here.

The stone bridge near the parking area is Bubble Pond Bridge, one of sixteen bridges that John D. Rockefeller, Jr. had commissioned for his Carriage Roads. At one point the Park Loop Road traveled under Bubble Pond Bridge, but it was eventually rerouted to create less of a disturbance near the pond.

Eagle Lake

As you continue driving, you'll see Eagle Lake at the bottom of the valley to your left. Eagle Lake is the largest body of water on the eastern half of the island. If you're lucky you might catch a glimpse one of the lake's feathered namesakes overhead. In the 1880s a privately run cog railway carried visitors to the top of Cadillac Mountain. To reach the railway, Passengers would board the steamship *Wauwinnet* at the north end of Eagle Lake, which would then carry them to the base of the mountain. When the railroad went bankrupt in the 1890s, the ship was scuttled to the bottom of Eagle Lake where it still rests to this day.

Legend of the Bubbles

According to a Wabanaki legend, the mountains known as the Bubbles were the result of a tremendous struggle between good and evil. As a virtuous god stood on Sargent Mountain on the left, a god of evil faced him from Pemetic on the right. A battle soon broke out that lasted for days. Finally the virtuous god asserted his dominance and forced his opponent off the top of Pemetic. Falling towards the waters of Jordan Pond, the evil god managed to grab onto the side of a cliff. As he clung to the ledge, two enormous boulders suddenly ripped free, pushing him down the mountain and burying him under their weight. Those two giant boulders make up the Bubbles we see today.

Sunset on Cadillac Mountain

⑲ Cadillac Mountain 22.3 miles

This is the final stop on the Park Loop Road. A 3.5-mile road ascends to the summit of the island's highest mountain, providing 360 degree views of the Maine coast. The road starts off to the right, so stay in the right lane as you approach it.

As you climb the Cadillac Mountain Road, you'll catch glimpses of Eagle Lake to the west and Bar Harbor and the Porcupine Islands to the east. There's a parking area at the top with a gift shop, restrooms, and fresh water. Looking west from the top of Cadillac, you can see the town of Blue Hill on the mainland with Swans Island and Isle au Haut out toward the horizon. On a clear day, you might be able to catch a glimpse of Katahdin, Maine's tallest mountain, 110 miles to the northwest.

During the 1800s Cadillac was called Green Mountain. The name was later changed as a historical reference to Antoine Laumet, the self-titled Sieur de Cadillac. In 1883 a large hotel was built on top of Cadillac Mountain, providing lodging and meals for visitors to Mount Desert. A private cog railway was constructed to bring guests to the top, but the venture went bankrupt after only a few years. Although the hotel was ultimately torn down, the abandoned railroad ties are still visible in some places.

Sunrise and sunset are both popular events at the top of Cadillac. Because of its elevation, the peak of Cadillac is the first spot in the United States to see the rays of the sun. Each evening in the summer, hordes of visitors are drawn to Cadillac to watch the spectacular sunsets over Eagle Lake. Parking can get tight. If you go, plan on arriving a bit early.

carriage roads

THE BRAINCHILD OF JOHN D. ROCKEFELLER, JR., the Carriage Road network is one of the jewels of Acadia and one of the most unique features in the national park system. Originally designed for horse enthusiasts as a refuge from the automobile, today over 57 miles of paved gravel roads wind their way through the heart of the Park, opening up hidden forest stretches to hikers and bikers, as well as horse riders. Scattered throughout this network are sixteen individually designed stone bridges that look like something out of a medieval fairy tale. Whether on foot, on bike, or on horse, the Carriage Roads are one aspect of Acadia that you don't want to miss.

From its northernmost terminus at Paradise Hill in Bar Harbor, the system extends south to the Rockefeller family estate in Seal Harbor, which is privately owned but left open to public use. Along the way the roads twist and wind around Eagle Lake, Jordan Pond, and Sargent Mountain, moving over brooks and past cascading waterfalls. The entire network of Carriage Roads is located on the eastern side of Mount Desert and does not extend farther east than Cadillac Mountain. Although the interconnecting series of roads can be a little bit confusing at first, using the numbered signposts found at the intersections with the maps on the following pages, you should have no problem navigating the roads like a pro.

A section of the Carriage Roads overlooking Jordan Pond

History of the Carriage Roads

IN 1837 A WOODEN BRIDGE was built connecting Mount Desert Island to the mainland. At the time it received wide acclaim - for the first time passage to the island did not require the use of a boat. While the construction of such a bridge was inevitable, its enormous impact on island life would not be felt for several decades to come.

When Henry Ford introduced the Model T to the masses in 1908, autos had already been banned on Mount Desert for several years. Not only were horse-powered forms of transportation favored, they were celebrated as a vital component of summer life. The annual Bar Harbor horse show was one of the island's most popular events. Banning autos served two purposes: wealthy summer visitors enjoyed the solace from modern life while year-round residents enjoyed limiting the pretentious lifestyles of wealthy visitors. All that changed with the introduction of the Model T. As the automobile craze swept the nation, local islanders were determined not to be left out of the fun. In 1909 a group of year-round residents attempted to repeal the ban on automobiles. Irritated by this sudden turn of events, wealthy summer visitors formed a political coalition and defeated the measure. Undaunted by such stiff opposition, the year-round residents vowed to take up matter once again when the State Legislature reconvened in two years.

Realizing that momentum in favor of automobiles was building, a group of summer residents met in New York City to form a plan of action. Determined to maintain the peaceful island life that attracted them in the first place, the group hired an aggressive legal team to lobby for their cause.

For out they turned, the summer folk, and when the count they wrote,
They'd kept the autos out of town by an enormous vote,
So glory hallelujah, hip, hip, and three times three;
Mount Desert Town of fair renown, from autos will be free.

-Herbert Weir Scythe, 1913

When the matter was taken up again, a temporary compromise was reached limiting the use of autos to the area surrounding Bar Harbor. When an island resident died because his horse drawn carriage did not reach the hospital in time, the repeal of the ban was a forgone conclusion. In 1915 automobiles were allowed in every town on Mount Desert. By that time there were nearly three-quarters of a million Model T's on American roads.

Carriage Road junction

But just because automobiles were allowed on the island didn't mean the summer residents had to like them. Among the most upset was John D. Rockefeller, Jr. At a time when virtually every wealthy Manhattan businessman arrived at work in a car, Rockefeller continued to commute via horse-drawn carriage. This quirky habit spoke volumes about his ill fit among the office buildings of downtown New York. Since day one John Jr. had been raised to take over the family business, and beginning in 1901 John Sr. began to cede control of the Standard Oil Corporation to his son. It was hardly a match made in heaven. Happiest outdoors, John Jr. would cope with the stress of office life by ordering twenty-foot logs delivered to the family stable where he would chop them into firewood after work. A few years after taking the helm at Standard Oil, John Jr. decided to abandon his post to devote himself full-time to philanthropic activities.

The same year that Rockefeller retired from corporate life, he purchased a cottage on Mount Desert. At this point the Great Automobile War - as it was later dubbed by local historians - was just beginning. Determined to enjoy the simple pleasure of a quiet carriage ride,

Although built as a refuge from the automobile, the carriage roads were funded by the Rockefeller oil fortune which, ironically, was made possible by the popular explosion of the auto-mobile. Further adding to this irony is the fact that the Ford family also summered on Mount Desert.

Rockefeller began building a series of gravel roads on his Seal Harbor property. As his network of individual roads started to grow, he decided to connect them in a continuous loop. But to do so required passing through land that had been set aside by the Hancock County Trustees of Public Reservations, the forefathers of Acadia National Park. When Rockefeller tried to purchase the land, his offer was refused. But the Trustees did tell him that if he wanted to build his connecting road with the knowledge that it might one day be shut down, he was allowed to do so. Rockefeller accepted this condition and construction commenced.

When word of Rockefeller's road leaked out, local residents grew alarmed. Conservationists feared that any man-made development would permanently scar the face of the Park. Among the most outspoken was Northeast Harbor resident George Wharton Pepper, who wrote to Rockefeller, "In my judgement it would be a serious mistake to extend your well conceived system of roads into this area." Rockefeller reluctantly ceased all construction underway.

Savy park supporter George Dorr recognized Rockefeller's enthusiasm for road building, and not wishing to lose a powerful ally in the effort to acquire additional land, suggested that Rockefeller might consider building an "access" road next to Jordan Pond. The idea excited Rockefeller

Courtesy National Park Service

Bridge construction

and he immediately hired a survey team to explore the possibilities. By 1921 the access road had expanded to include a series of roads that connected to his own. Although officially the new Carriage Roads were ordered by George Dorr, it was Rockefeller who studied and planned them, simply making "suggestions" as to where they might be placed. Stories of Rockefeller's hands-on involvement with the minutia of road construction are legendary. Rockefeller didn't just want a network of Carriage Roads, he wanted to create them. Always in contact with his teams of surveyors and engineers, Rockefeller was a constant presence on the construction sites.

When local residents figured out what was going on, resistance to the roads once again surfaced. Although they admittedly approved of the small network already in place, residents felt that further construction would be a terrible mistake. Again it was Northeast Harbor resident George Pepper - by this time a senator from Pennsylvania - who led the charge. Pepper used his influence to convince the Secretary of the Interior to order a halt to all road construction within the boundaries of the Park.

But by this time Rockefeller's grand vision of a vast network of roads running through the Park was firmly in place. Working with Dorr, he proceeded to build yet another series of Carriage Roads near Eagle Lake on lands that had not yet officially been added to the Park. Again a cry of protest went out, but this time there was nothing that could be legally done to stop them.

Attempting to sooth the heated debate, Dorr personally invited Secretary of the Interior Hubert Work to Mount Desert to check out the Carriage Roads firsthand. In the summer of 1924, Work arrived on the

How Much Was Rockefeller Really Worth?

In 1913, shortly before the government breakup of the Standard Oil Company, the Rockefeller family fortune was valued at 900 million dollars. So how much would that be worth today? Applying changes in the Consumer Price Index, that works out to about $15 billion in 2000 dollars. But looking at Rockefeller's fortune as a proportion of the 1913 Gross National Product provides a measure of the overall economic clout he wielded at the time. By that standard Rockefeller would be worth roughly $212 billion dollars today, over twice the value of Microsoft's Bill Gates.

Construction of Duck Brook Bridge

island and was pleasantly surprised by what he saw. He immediately issued an approval of all previously completed Carriage Roads that made them a permanent addition to the Park. Furthermore, he would allow Rockefeller to continue building roads as long as they were approved by his office first. The most significant obstacle to the completion of the Carriage Roads had been overcome.

In 1928 construction was approved for a series of roads around Witch Hole Pond and Paradise Hill outside of Bar Harbor. At this point, expansion of the Carriage Roads stopped, and for the next ten years Rockefeller focused on connecting the individual roads into a single continuous network. By 1940 the system was complete.

When Rockefeller first started building his Carriage Roads, horse-drawn transportation was still a popular component of island life. By 1940 it had turned into a quaint hobby for those that could afford it. At the same time bicycle use had taken off in America. Rockefeller was keenly aware of this fact and was one of the first proponents to open the Carriage Roads to bicycle use. For over 60 years a wide range of outdoor enthusiasts have enjoyed exploring the one of a kind Carriage Roads. With the help of an eight-million dollar endowment established in 1990, Rockefeller's personal gift to the visitors of Mount Desert will continue to be enjoyed for years to come.

The Carriage Road Bridges

SIXTEEN INDIVIDUAL stone bridges lay scattered throughout the Carriage Road system. Each one of these bridges took over a full year to construct. Employing local contractors and stonemasons, Rockefeller spared no expense to produce bridges of the highest possible quality that would blend naturally with the

local environment. New York architect Welles Bosworth was responsible for the design of most of the early bridges, but after World War I he was sent to Paris to direct the restoration of Versailles, Fontainebleau, and Rheims Cathedral - an undertaking made financially possible by Rockefeller. Charles Stoughton, a New York architect who had designed bridges for the Bronx River Parkway, was called in to work on the remaining bridges. Each Carriage Road bridge has the date of construction marked somewhere in the stone. But just as no two designs are alike, each date is placed in a different location.

Duck Brook Bridge today

Exploring the Carriage Roads

The following pages outline the four major sections of the Carriage Road network. The Witch Hole Pond region is generally considered to be the easiest section while the westernmost roads of the Hadlock Pond Region offer the most challenging terrain. But whatever your level of activity, there are great views and fantastic sights throughout the carriage road system. Decades of planning went into the layout of these roads, and it is hard to find a section that isn't a treat to explore.

Horse Drawn Carriage Rides

Wildwood Stables, off the Park Loop Road near Seal Harbor, offers horse drawn carriage rides around the Carriage Roads. These rides are a great way to enjoy the Carriage Roads in the context in which they were originally intended. Several rides are offered during the day - their most popular is the Day Mountain sunset ride, which offers stunning ocean views. Stop by Wildwood Stables for more information or call 207-276-3622

Carriage Road Rules

- Carriage Roads are two-way. Stay to the right, pass on the left.
- Move to the side of the road when stopping.
- Pets are allowed on the carriage roads but must be leashed.
- Bicycles and horses are not allowed on hiking trails that sometimes cross the Carriage Roads.
- Hikers and bikers must yield to horses, bikers must yield to hikers.
- Use caution when approaching horses, slow down if you are on a bike and give warning if you are approaching from behind. Frightened horses can sometimes act unpredictably.

Carriage Road Tips

- Although not required, helmets are advised.
- Bring plenty of water.
- Pay attention to where you are. The carriage trails can get confusing, especially around Jordan Pond. Use the maps in this book and the numbered signposts at carriage trail intersections to determine where you are.

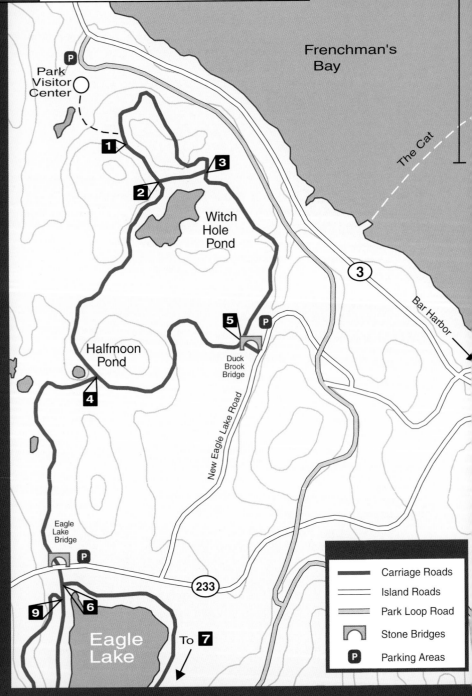

Witch Hole Pond

N

1 mile

Frenchman's Bay

P

Park Visitor Center

The Cat

1

2

3

Witch Hole Pond

3

Bar Harbor →

5

P

Duck Brook Bridge

Halfmoon Pond

4

New Eagle Lake Road

Eagle Lake Bridge

P

233

9

6

Eagle Lake

To **7**

	Carriage Roads
	Island Roads
	Park Loop Road
	Stone Bridges
P	Parking Areas

Witch Hole Pond

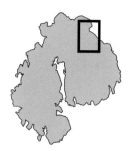

The Witch Hole Pond region's close proximity to Bar Harbor and easy-to-moderate terrain make this one of the most popular sections of carriage roads to explore - keep in mind that in July and August the roads here can become a bit congested. No horses are allowed in this region and it is predominantly used by bikers, but the fine gravel and smooth roads are well suited for wheelchairs and strollers.

Highlights

Paradise Hill - offers terrific views of Frenchman's Bay.

Duck Brook Bridge - this triple arch bridge towers over Duck Brook and is one of the most photographed bridges in the Carriage Road system. Note that there are stairs that lead to the base of the bridge on the southern side.

Witch Hole Pond - home to a wide range of animal life. If you're lucky, you might catch a glimpse of the ducks or beavers that frequent Witch Hole Pond.

Most Popular Route

5 - 3 - 1 - 2 - 4 - 5

Eagle Lake

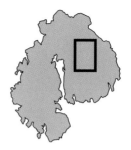

The Eagle Lake region opens up a part of Acadia National Park that is only accessible by Carriage Roads. This is the most inland section of the system. It combines lake and pondside rides with fascinating views of the mountains overhead. Note that swimming is prohibited in both Eagle Lake and Bubble Pond since they are both public water supplies.

Highlights

Eagle Lake - the largest body of water on the eastern half of the island. The roads that skirt the shores of Eagle Lake provide peaceful and serene riding experiences.

Bubble Pond - this small pond rests in the glacially carved valley between Cadillac and Pemetic Mountains. Loons are fond of Bubble Pond and their haunting call can sometimes be heard near the shore.

Aunt Betty Pond - this small pond and the marshy areas that surround it offer an enjoyable destination, but be forewarned that no matter what way you choose to get there, you're in for a long and tiring ride uphill.

Most Popular Routes

6 - 8 - 7 - 6
6 - 9 - 11 - 10 - 8 - 6
7 - 8 - 10 - 14 - 15 - 16 - 17 - 7

Hadlock Ponds

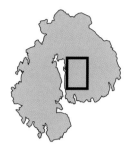

The sometimes steep and challenging terrain of the Hadlock Pond region offers some of the most unique carriage road scenery in the system. The workout you'll receive is rewarded with elevated lookouts and dramatic stone bridges.

Highlights

Waterfall Bridge - positioned next to a steep drop-off by Hadlock Brook. If it hasn't rained in a while, this waterfall is really more of a trickle, but within several days of a downpour, the cascading water and stunning bridge is a great sight.

Deer Brook Bridge - passes over Deer Brook just north of elevated views of the upper half of Jordan Pond.

Giant Slide - refers to the section of roads between signposts 10 and 12. Giant slide passes along the edge of Sargent and Parkman mountains, providing great views of Somes Sound, Blue Hill Bay, the Camden Hills, and the Gulf of Maine.

Amphitheater Bridge - wrapping sharply around the steep valley between Penobscot and Cedar Swamp Mountains, the Amphitheater Bridge is located in a wonderfully secluded section of the Carriage Roads.

Brown Mountain Gatehouse - located off route 3 near post 18, the Brown Mountain Gatehouse was designed as one of two checked entry points to keep automobiles off the Carriage Roads.

Most Popular Routes

18 - 19 - 12 - 13 - 18
18 - 19 - 20 - 21 - 22 - 20 - 19 - 18
18 - 19 - 20 - 22 - 21 - 14 - 10 - 12 - 19 - 18

Jordan Pond

3

Day Mtn

37

17

To 7

38

Stanley Brook Road

To Seal Harbor

30

29

31

P

P

27

25

16

26

28

Jordan Pond

15

23

14

24

Little Long Pond

West Branch Bridge

Cliffside Bridge

Cobblestone Bridge

32

22

21

To 10

Amphitheater Bridge

Little Harbor Brook Bridge

20

To 19

Carriage Roads

Island Roads

Park Loop Road

Stone Bridges

P Parking Area

N

1 mile

Jordan Pond

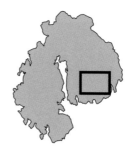

The Jordan Pond region offers moderate biking that passes alongside bubbling streams, forest groves, and up coastal lookouts. This is another high traffic area that sees heavy use in July and August. Note that portions of the Jordan Pond region lie on the Rockefeller family's private land and are not open to bicycle use. The roads south of signposts 22, 24, 28, and 31are closed to bikers, but can still be enjoyed by hikers, horse riders, and cross country skiers.

Highlights

Day Mountain - more of a hill than a mountain, this offers sweeping views of Great Harbor and the Cranberry Isles. Wildwood Stables offers daily sunset rides up Day Mountain, so if you choose to explore it during this time, watch out for approaching carriages around the hairpin turns.

Jordan Stream - between signposts 15 and 23. This fabulous stretch skirts the crystal clear shores of Jordan Stream. Coasting down hill from signpost 15 is a great way to take it in.

Jordan Pond Gatehouse - This French Romanesque building was built in 1932. See page 65.

Most Popular Routes

16 - 15 - 23 - 25 - 16
16 - 17 - 37 - 36 - up Day Mtn - 38 - 37 - 17 - 16
16 - 15 - 14 - 21 - 22 - 20 - 21 - 14 - 15 - 16

hiking

Hiking In Acadia National Park

Mount Desert Island's unique mountain landscape lends itself to some of the finest coastal hiking in the world. There are trails up every mountain, many offering sweeping views of both the island interior and the coast of Maine. Each year thousands of tourists visit Acadia without ever stepping foot on a trail. Don't be that tourist! There are 130 miles of fantastic hikes all over the island for people of all ages and abilities, so you have no excuse not to get out there. Even if you only have time to squeeze in one quick hike on your vacation, it's worth it.

How to use this guide

The trail descriptions below provide brief summaries of 23 of the most popular trails in Acadia. A series of comprehensive maps containing additional trails have also been included on the following pages. Acadia's trail system is consistently well marked and easy to follow. Blue blazes and cairns (rock piles) placed by park personnel mark all of the paths. If you have a good sense of direction and even just a little common sense, you should have no problem navigating the trails.

Top Five Hikes

Although it's hard to single out a handful of trails as "the best," the following trails are consistently popular.

- Acadia Mountain
- The Beehive
- Penobscot Mountain
- Precipice Trail (Champlain Mtn)
- South Ridge Trail (Cadillac Mtn)

Jessup Path

What to expect on the trails

Many trails have been altered to make them safer and more accessible. It is not uncommon to find stone stairs, iron rungs, and ladders on any given trail. Although some of these may appear old and rickety, rest assured that park officials carefully monitor their durability to bring you the safest and best hike possible.

Blue blaze

Cairn

Iron rungs

National Park Service Ratings

Easy: Level ground.

Moderate: Uneven ground with some steep sections. Footing can be difficult.

Strenuous: Steep climbing with some difficult footing and maneuvering

Ladder: The most difficult hikes. Iron ladders and rungs are used to get through particularly steep sections.

Hiking Tips

- Wear good shoes (preferably hiking boots) and bring plenty of water.
- Dress in layers. Temperatures can rapidly change.
- If possible, wear synthetics. Cotton is infamous for its water absorption and can cool you down. If you don't have synthetics, don't worry about it. Early hikers didn't have them either.
- Follow blue blazes (on trees and rocks) and cairns. If you think you might have wandered off the path, consult the maps and then back track to the last definite marking.
- Trail difficulty ratings: Unless you consider yourself badly out of shape, chances are you can hike any trail on the island. But you know your limits so you must use your own discretion.
- Children: Don't use trail difficulty ratings to decide whether or not to bring children on a hike. Use the children in question to decide whether or not to bring them. Some kids get bored on anything less than a straight ascent while others probably won't be able to handle a hike until they're 30. You know your kids better than the person who rated the trail.
- Dogs are allowed on trails but must be leashed.

A Brief History of Acadia's Trails

Native American trails had been in existence on Mount Desert for centuries before modern trail building began. Used primarily for hunting and reaching mountain lookouts, many provided the early framework for the trails as we know them today. When summer visitors started arriving in the mid 1800s, hiking became one of the most popular outdoor activities. Each town on Mount Desert established their own Village Improvement Associations to upgrade the existing trails and create new ones. Soon a kind of friendly competition broke out among towns to see who could build the best trails. Flush with money from wealthy summer residents, trail construction flourished. In the 1930s the Army's Civilian Conservation Corps added trails to provide employment opportunities during the Great Depression. Although the basic network of trails has remained the same for decades, heavy use and natural wear and tear have taken their toll. In 1999 a $15 million endowment was established to ensure that Acadia's hiking trails will be cared for and properly maintained in perpetuity.

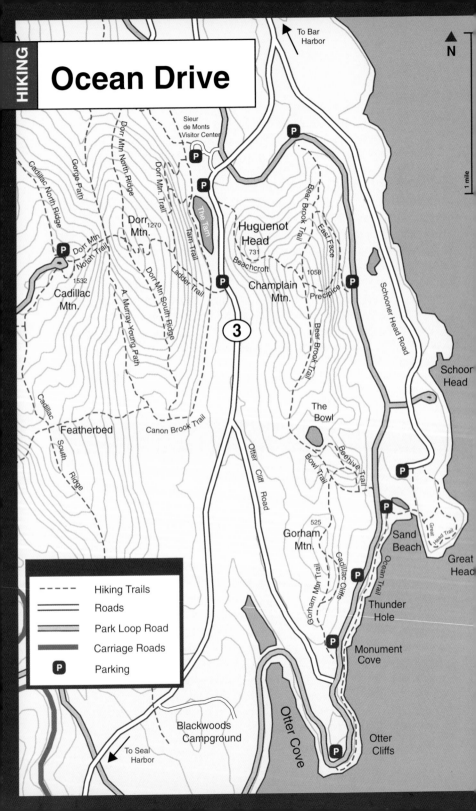

Ocean Drive Region

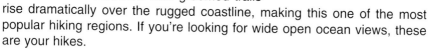

Ocean Drive refers to the stretch of the Park Loop Road that skirts the eastern shores of Mount Desert. Well groomed trails rise dramatically over the rugged coastline, making this one of the most popular hiking regions. If you're looking for wide open ocean views, these are your hikes.

Beehive
NPS rating: Ladder

Probably the most popular hike on the island. The Beehive rises sharply above Sand Beach providing some of the best coastal views of any trail. If you've got a limited amount of time but know you want to squeeze in at least one dramatic hike, this is your best bet. The shortest loop is only a mile and a half. Be forewarned that there are a few precarious spots. Although not technically challenging, the drop-offs are steep and can be a bit intimidating for some people. The trail starts across from the Sand Beach parking area.

If you hate great hikes and spectacular views, the Beehive is not for you...

Enjoying the view from the top of Champlain

Champlain Mountain via the Beachcroft Path
NPS rating: Moderate

If the steep drop-offs of The Precipice aren't your thing, you can still enjoy the sweeping views from the top of Champlain via the Beachcroft Trail. Starting across from the parking area on route 3, the Beachcroft heads up an impressive set of stone stairs overlooking the marshy pond known as the Tarn. It then dips between Huguenot Head and the peak of Champlain. For a little variation on the way down, you can take the Bear Brook Trail: but to loop back to the parking area, you'll have to take a long and somewhat boring stroll along the Park Loop Road.

Gorham Mountain
NPS rating: Moderate

Rising above one of the most dramatic sections of the Park Loop Road this is a quick and easy hike with many wide-open views. Often favored by family hikers looking for a good hike that's not too challenging. The trail starts at the parking area across from Monument Cove on the Park Loop Road. For an extended hike keep on going past the summit of Gorham Mountain and take the Bowl Trail down to the Park Loop Road. Soon you can pick up the Ocean Trail that skirts the shoreline, bringing you back to the parking area.

Great Head
NPS rating: Moderate

A short but sweet hike that wraps around the jagged rocks of Great Head. The Great Head Trail starts at the east end of Sand Beach not far from the lagoon. As the trail turns inland and reaches the highpoint of Great Head (145 feet), you'll find the stone remains of an old teahouse that was once owned by the daughter of J.P. Morgan.

Ocean Trail
NPS rating: Easy

This is a great way to really take in the scenery of the Park Loop Road instead of having it blow past you in a car. The trail starts in the Sand Beach Parking area near the stairs that descend to the beach and continues along the shore all the way to Otter Cliffs.

Precipice
NPS rating: Ladder

Winding its way up one of the steepest cliffs on Mount Desert, the narrow walkways and steep drop-offs make this the most famous hike in Acadia. This is the most direct route to the top of Champlain Mountain. The trail is usually closed from May to September to protect nesting peregrine falcons, but if you happen to be here when the trail is open, you should seriously consider this hike, if not for the dramatic views, at least for the bragging rights. It is steep and it can get a bit slippery after a recent rain, but it takes more mental strength than physical strength to conquer The Precipice. If you are terrified of heights, you should find a different trail. Otherwise go for it. The Precipice Trail starts at the base of Champlain Mtn. next to the parking area off the Park Loop Road.

Bar Harbor Region

Trails up both Cadillac and Dorr Mountain lie only a short distance away from Bar Harbor and offer great views of both the island's interior and th coast beyond. Although challenging, trails going up or down the jagged notch between the two mountains offer truly impressive views.

Cadillac Mountain North Ridge
NPS rating: Moderate

With great views of Bar Harbor, the Porcupine Islands, and Eagle Lake, this trail offers a gradual and satisfying ascent to the top of Mount Desert's highest peak. The trail starts across from a small parking area on the Park Loop Road. At times the trail comes close to, but never crosses, the motor road up Cadillac Mountain. Impatient hikers may feel a bit taunted by the steady stream of cars heading up the mountain, but you will feel nothing but pure satisfaction when you reach the top and realize you are one of the proud and the few that actually reached the top via human locomotion. From here you can go back the way you came or turn the hike into a strenuous loop following the Dorr Notch Trail down, then heading north on the Gorge Trail.

Cadillac Mountain West Face Trail
NPS rating: Strenuous

Starting across a small footbridge at the north end of Bubble Pond, the West Face Trail is the shortest route to the summit. Backtracking on the way down, take the South Ridge Trail until it meets up with the Pond Trail. Take the Pond Trail down to the Bubble Pond Carriage Road and follow it back to the parking area.

Ladder Trail
NPS rating: Ladder

A quintessential Acadian hike. This has virtually every element of what you can expect to find hiking on Mount Desert. Stone stairs, iron rungs, a shaky ladder, mountain valleys and coastal views. They're all here. On the way down you can either choose the Dorr Mtn. South Ridge trail or continue down the west side of Dorr Mountain and follow the A. Murray Young path. The latter is a longer route but a great hike along a bubbling stream. The best way to get to the Ladder Trail is from the parking area south of the Tarn off route 3.

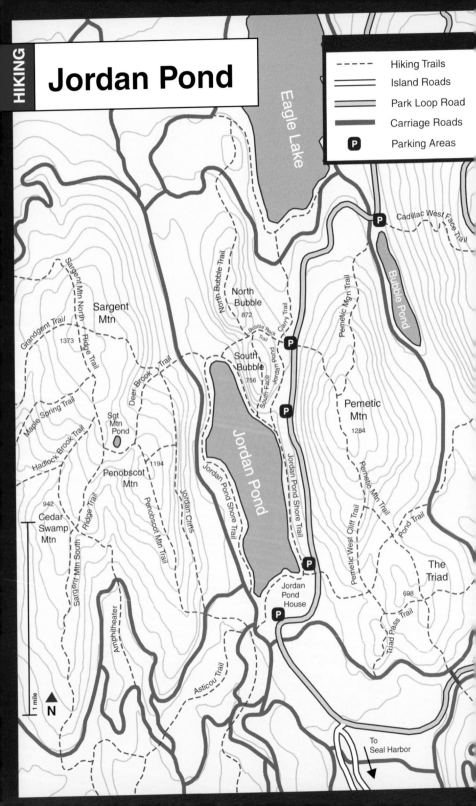

Jordan Pond Region

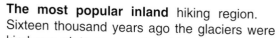

The most popular inland hiking region.
Sixteen thousand years ago the glaciers were
kind enough to carve out a wide range of hiking here with towering views of
Jordan Pond and the southern shores of Mount Desert.

The Bubbles
NPS rating: Moderate

Sure everybody raves about the view of the Bubbles from the Jordan Pond
House, but it's a little known secret that the view back is even more spectacular. Hiking along both North and South Bubble will give you great views
of both Jordan Pond to the south and Eagle Lake to the north. Follow the
Bubble Rock Trail that runs perpendicular to the Park Loop Road. Then
head over to South Bubble to check out 16 ton Bubble Rock up close.

The Bubbles South Face
NPS rating: Strenuous

What this trail lacks in ease, it makes up for in dramatic views Be prepared
to pass steep drop- offs and possible loose footing on the way up, but once
you reach the top, it's all moderate hiking around the Bubbles. To get to the
South Face Trail, park next to the Bubble Rock Trail then follow the Jordan
Pond Carry Trail south. Take a right when you reach the Jordan Pond Shore
Trail. The beginning of the South Face Trail will be on your right.

Jordan Cliffs
NPS Rating: Ladder

Like The Precipice this is a steep climb with great views. Also like the
Precipice its usually closed from May to September due to nesting
Peregrine falcons. But when it is open, the Jordan Cliffs Trail is one of the
best ways to get to the top of Penobscot Mountain. The trail starts near the
spot where the Penobscot Mtn. Trail intersects a section of the Carriage
Roads - see page 105. Signs should indicate whether or not the trail is
open. Be prepared for some slippery spots if it has recently rained.

Hiking The Bubbles South Face

Jordan Pond Shore Trail
NPS rating: Moderate

For the most part this is a very easy trail that skirts the peaceful shores of Jordan Pond forming a continuous loop. However there are a few boulder sections where the footing gets a little tricky, hence the moderate rating. You can pick up the trail in front of the Jordan Pond House or near the parking area a little north on the Park Loop Road. Parking can get more than a little tight near the Jordan Pond house in July and August, so unless you're a hiker and a diner, you should park at the northern parking area.

Pemetic Mountain
NPS rating: Strenuous

Like Penobscot Mountain this is a trail with great views of Jordan Pond and the southern shore of the island with the added bonus of elevated views of Frenchman's Bay, Seal Harbor, and sections of Ocean Drive along the Park Loop Road. The best place to start this hike is half a mile north of the Jordan Pond House just off the Park Loop Road. Follow the Pemetic West Cliff Trail. Easy at first, the trail gets more challenging as you go higher and higher. Once at the top, the best ways down are either heading back the way you came or continuing the trail down to Bubble Pond and looping back along the nearby Carriage Road.

Penobscot Mountain Trail
NPS Rating: Strenuous

Rising over the western shore of Jordan Pond, the Penobscot Mountain Trail rises above the treeline to provide sweeping views of Jordan Pond, the interior of the island, and its southern shore. To begin this trail, head west across the lawn behind the Jordan Pond House (near the public restrooms). Signs will direct you to the trail. When you reach a section of the Carriage Roads, cross the footbridge to the right and continue straight along the path. Once you reach the top, you can turn back or continue on to Sargent Mountain, the second highest peak on the island.

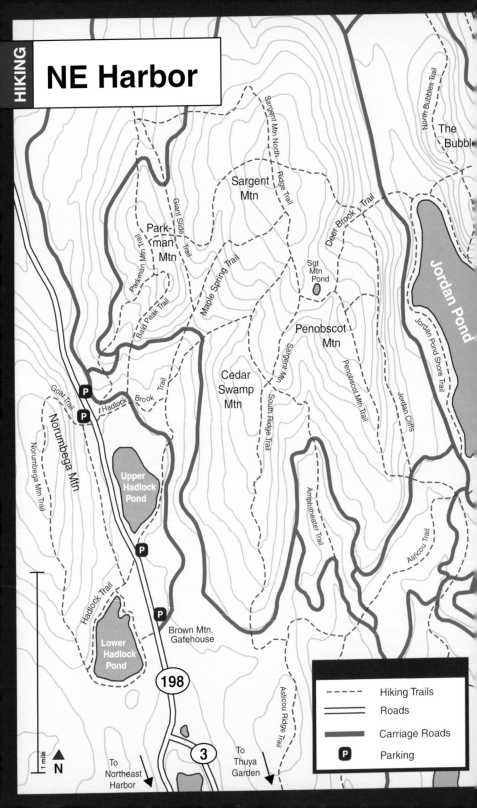

NE Harbor

Sargent Mtn

Park-man Mtn

Penobscot Mtn

Cedar Swamp Mtn

Norumbega Mtn

Jordan Pond

The Bubbl

Sgt Mtn Pond

Upper Hadlock Pond

Lower Hadlock Pond

Brown Mtn. Gatehouse

North Bubbles Trail

Sargent Mtn North Ridge Trail

Deer Brook Trail

Giant Slide Trail

Parkman Mtn Trail

Bald Peak Trail

Maple Spring Trail

Jordan Pond Shore Trail

Sargent Mtn South Ridge Trail

Penobscot Mtn Trail

Jordan Cliffs

Goat Trail

Hadlock Brook Trail

Norumbega Mtn Trail

Hadlock Trail

Ampitheater Trail

Asticou Trail

Asticou Ridge Trail

198

3

To Northeast Harbor

To Thuya Garden

1 mile

N

	Hiking Trails
	Roads
	Carriage Roads
P	Parking

NE Harbor Region

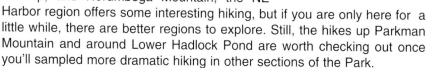

Defined here as Sargent, Parkman, Cedar Swamp, and Norumbega Mountain, the NE Harbor region offers some interesting hiking, but if you are only here for a little while, there are better regions to explore. Still, the hikes up Parkman Mountain and around Lower Hadlock Pond are worth checking out once you'll sampled more dramatic hiking in other sections of the Park.

Parkman Mountain
NPS rating: Ladder

This is a quick hike that offers great views of Somes Sound and Northeast Harbor. The best route up starts near the parking area just north of Upper Hadlock Pond. Follow the Hadlock Brook Trail that starts across the street until you reach the Maple Spring Trail that veers off to the left. Take your next left onto the Giant Slide Trail and after a little while take another left towards the peak of Parkman Mountain. From the top you have your choice of routes back to the parking area. The Penobscot Mtn. Trail is considered the easier of the two.

Sargent Mountain via the Maple Spring Trail
NPS Rating: Strenuous

Samuel Champlain was probably staring at Sargent Mountain when he named the island *L'isle des Monts Deserts* "Island of Barren Mountains". The lack of vegetation near the peak makes for great views of the north side of the island and the mainland beyond. Park at the base of Norumbega Mtn. and follow the Hadlock Brook Trail to the Maple Spring Trail.

Lower Hadlock Pond
NPS Rating: Easy

This is an quick and easy hike that wraps around the quiet shores of Lower Hadlock Pond, passing by a private, fairy tale house painted entirely pink and over a small footbridge that passes over a gushing stream. You can pick up the trail across from the Brown Mountain Carriage Road Gatehouse.

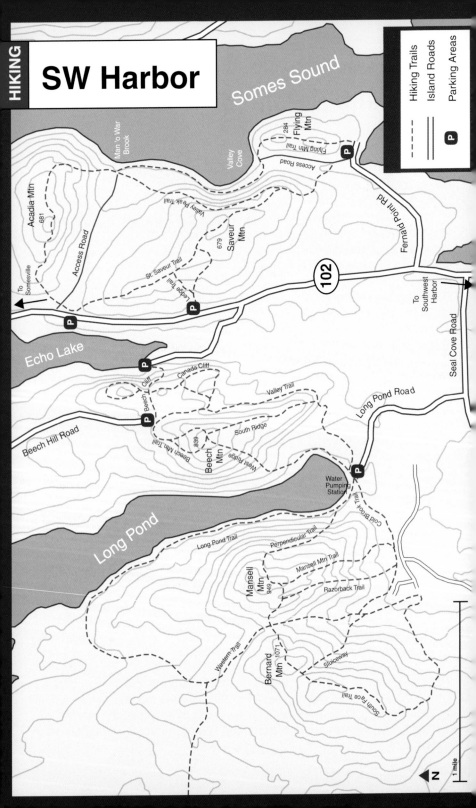

SW Harbor

Somes Sound

Man 'o War Brook

Valley Cove

284 Flying Mtn

Flying Mtn Trail

Access Road

Access Road

Acadia Mtn
681

Valley Peak Trail

Saveur Mtn
679

St. Saveur Trail

Ledge Trail

Fernald Point Rd

To Somesville

102

To Southwest Harbor

Seal Cove Road

Echo Lake

Canada Cliff

Beech Cliff

Valley Trail

Long Pond Road

Beech Hill Road

South Ridge

Beech Mtn
839

Beech Mtn Trail

West Ridge

Water Pumping Station

Cold Brook Trail

Long Pond

Long Pond Trail

Perpendicular Trail

Mansell Mtn Trail

Mansell Mtn
949

Razorback Trail

Western Trail

Bernard Mtn
1071

Sluiceway

South Face Trail

Hiking Trails

Island Roads

P Parking Areas

N

1 mile

SW Harbor Region

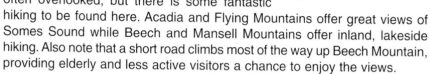

Because this region lies on the much less visited western side of the island, it is often overlooked, but there is some fantastic hiking to be found here. Acadia and Flying Mountains offer great views of Somes Sound while Beech and Mansell Mountains offer inland, lakeside hiking. Also note that a short road climbs most of the way up Beech Mountain, providing elderly and less active visitors a chance to enjoy the views.

Acadia Mountain
NPS rating: Moderate

Although a relatively low peak, Acadia Mountain offers spectacular views of Somes Sound. There's a parking area off Route 102 three miles south of Somesville. Across the road is the beginning of the trail. Head south on the Saint Sauveur trail and then making a counter-clockwise loop back toward Acadia Mtn. At the base of Acadia Mountain is Man o' War Brook, a cascading stream that empties into Somes Sound where 19th-century ships used to replenish their water supplies.

Looking out over Somes Sound from Acadia Mountain

Beech Mountain
NPS rating: Moderate

There are a number of ways you can get to the top of Beech Mountain, all are very rewarding. Probably the most popular way up is along the Beech Cliffs Trail (NPS: Ladder) starting at Echo Beach. This trail is short, steep, and sweet, although if iron ladders scare you, you should probably skip it. Another option is to start at the southern tip of Long Pond and head up the West Ridge Trail and loop back on the South Ridge Trail. At the top of Beech Mountain is a 30-foot high fire tower occasionally manned by Park volunteers.

*Note: Less active visitors can still enjoy the views along Beech Mountain. Beech Hill Road will take you to a parking area near the mountain's peak. From here you can either head east and check out Beech Cliffs, or head west and follow the loop around the tip of Beech Mountain. The Beech Mountain loop is slightly more demanding but if you do it be sure too bear right when the trail forks just west of the parking area - much better views. To get to Beech Hill Road, head west on Route 102 just south of Somesville. Take a left on Beech Hill Road and follow it up until you reach the parking area.

Flying Mountain Trail
NPS rating: Moderate

Named by Native Americans who felt that this peak appeared to be "flying" away from adjacent St. Sauveur Mountain. Like Acadia Mountain, this peak offers fantastic views of Somes Sound and overlooks Northeast Harbor, Southwest Harbor, and the Cranberry Isles beyond. To get to the start of the trail, turn onto Fernald Point Road just north of Southwest Harbor. Follow it most of the way down until you reach the Valley Cove Fire Road. A cedar post marks the beginning of the trial that rises quickly through spruce woods. Following the trail over the mountain you'll wind up at Valley Cove. This is a fantastic spot for a picnic. From here you can either take the wide access road back to the parking area, or continue along the shore and extend your hike.

Great Pond Trail
NPS rating: Easy

The most peaceful hike in Acadia. This relatively flat trail skirts the western edge of Long Pond for about a mile and a half before heading into the woods. Along the way you'll be treated to the sound of water gently lapping the rocks along the shore. Although swimming is prohibited near the pumping station, you can go for a dip anywhere you want after heading north on the trail for about a third of a mile. If you're looking for a long hike that offers some upward mobility, follow the trail into the woods and loop back to Mansell Mountain. Otherwise, head back the way you came. The Great Pond Trail starts next to the water pumping station. Use the same parking area as for the Perpendicular Trail.

Perpendicular Trail Mansell Mountain
NPS rating: Strenuous

One of the most unique and underhiked trails on the island. A winding stone staircase of biblical proportions heads up (or down if you prefer) the sheer face of Mount Mansell, providing great views of both Long Pond and the Cranberry Isles. There are a number of trails west of the peak of Mansell Mountain that lead back to the parking area. The Razorback Trail is quite popular. To get to the parking area, turn west onto Seal Cove Road off Route 102 just north of Southwest Harbor. Take your first right onto Long Pond Road and follow it until it ends at the water pumping station at the southern tip of Long Pond. There's a small parking to the right of the station. If it's full you can park on the shoulder of the road leading in.

schoodic
peninsula

Schoodic Peninsula

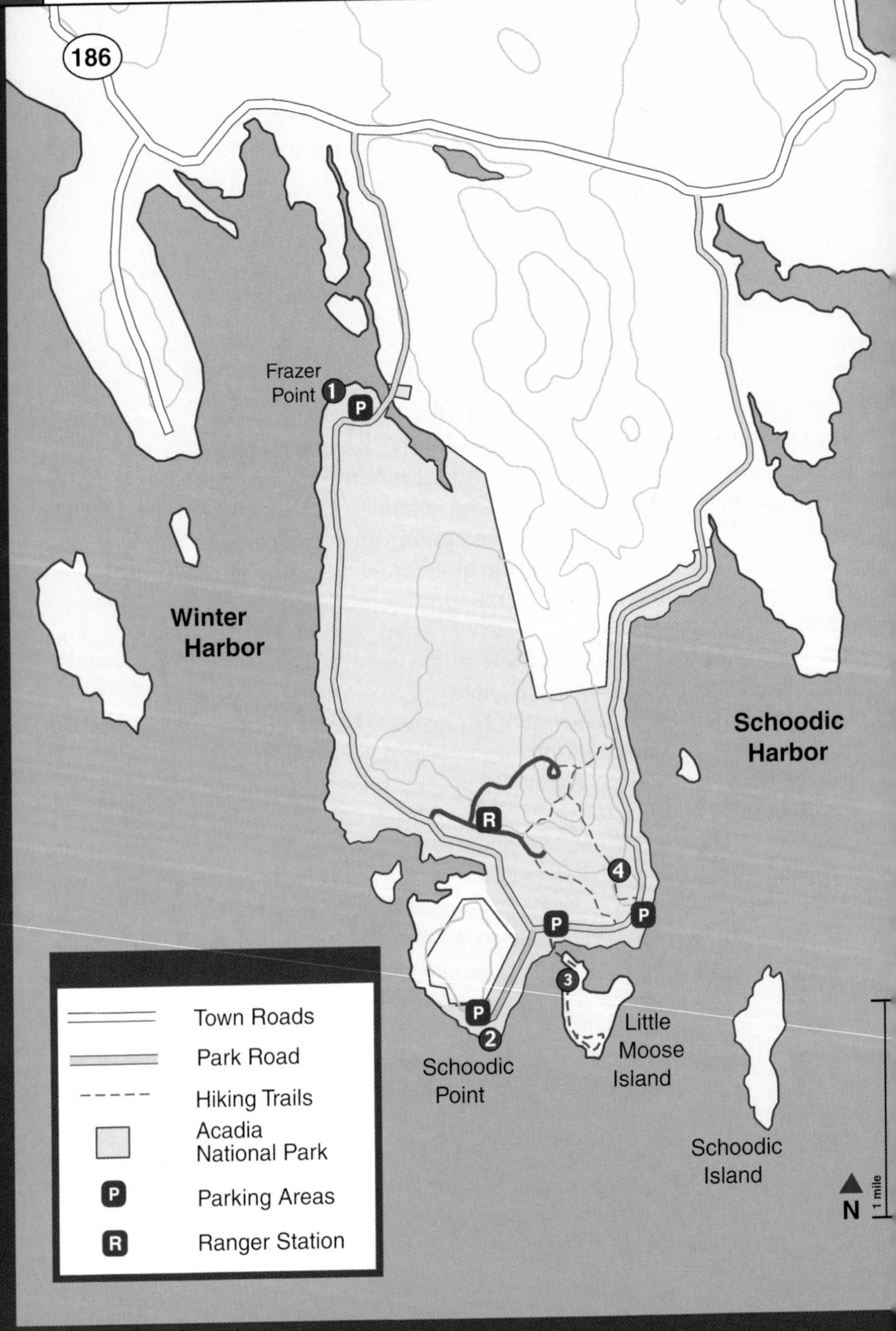

186

Frazer Point ❶ Ⓟ

Winter Harbor

Schoodic Harbor

Ⓡ

❹

Ⓟ   Ⓟ

❸

Little Moose Island

Ⓟ

❷

Schoodic Point

Schoodic Island

Town Roads

Park Road

Hiking Trails

Acadia National Park

Ⓟ   Parking Areas

Ⓡ   Ranger Station

▲
N   1 mile

❶ Frazer Point Picnic Area

This area contains several picnic tables and grills with a fantastic view over-looking Winter Harbor. There's also a pier where you can fish or just take in the scenery. If you're planning on biking the road around Schoodic, leave your car here and start your journey.

❷ Schoodic Point

After traveling along the western edge of the peninsula, you'll come upon a United States Navy Base. Unless you've got clearance, continue on the road and take a right on the two-way road to Schoodic Point. Here you can observe the dramatic wave action firsthand. During hurricanes rocks the size of grapefruits have been known to be tossed into the woods behind the parking area here.

❸ Little Moose Island

Like Bar Island in Bar Harbor, Little Moose Island is connected to the shore at low tide when a gravel sand bar is exposed. At this time adventurers can walk over to a small rocky beach on the western side of the island. If you do decide to go over to Little Moose Island, make sure you go before low tide hits to give yourself plenty of time to explore. From here you can head

Capturing Schoodic on canvas. Be aware that wave action is very unpredictable here. Use caution if you choose to step out onto the rocks.

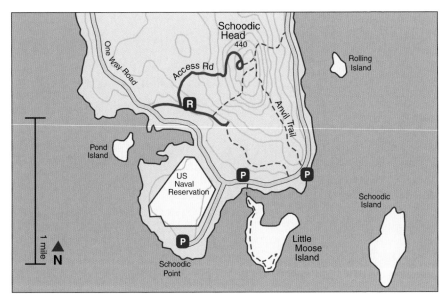

Hiking trails on Schoodic Peninsula

south on a small overgrown path that climbs from the beach. As you wander by the shore, keep your eyes out for groups of eider ducks bobbing in the waves. In the early 1900s a fashion craze for hats made from eider feathers swept the country and almost caused the birds' extinction. The hats sometimes included an entire bird mounted on the top. Protective legislation was later enacted that saved the birds.

❹ Anvil Trail

This 1-mile trail rises to the top of Schoodic Head, the highest point on the peninsula. From this point you can enjoy fantastic views of Winter Harbor and Mount Desert Island. To get there, continue about a mile past Schoodic Point on the one-way road. There's a small parking area on the right where you can park your car. The Anvil Trail starts across the road. Follow the blue blazes until you reach an overlook marked by a small rock cairn. After about a mile you'll reach an intersection with another trail. Bear right and continue on until you reach another junction. This time turn left. After about a tenth of a mile, you'll reach Schoodic Head. After soaking in the views, retrace your steps and head back to the parking area.

isle au
haut

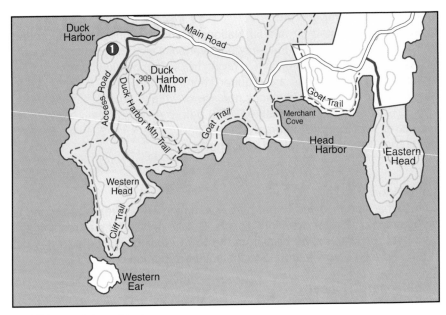

Hiking on Isle au Haut

Historic Register, this six-room inn is booked for months in advance with prices starting at $250 a night. Breakfast, lunch, and a candle light dinner are included. Two-night minimum. 207-367-2261

❹ Hiking

The network of hiking trails south of Duck Harbor is sometimes challenging, always rewarding. Bobbing in and out of dark spruce forests, the Western Head Trail and Cliff Trail skirt the shoreline and provide fantastic views of Isle au Haut's rugged coast. At low tide you can cross over to Western Ear Island near the junction of the two trails. Make sure you pay attention to the time, so you don't get stranded and obey all posted restrictions - the island is privately owned. The Goat Trail also passes near the shore and meets up with the Duck Harbor Mountain Trail, which, while challenging, provides great views from the mountain peak. Give yourself at least three hours for any loop from Duck Harbor to be safe. As you hike the trails, keep your eyes out for sweet ferns. Although not actually a real fern (even though they look like one), the sweet fern has been used to add scent to candles and soaps for centuries.

towns & villages

Bar Harbor

Legend:
- Town Roads
- Park Loop Road
- Hiking Trails
- **P** Parking Areas

Shore Path

Wayman Lane
Barberry Lane
Livingston Rd
Hospital
Hancock St
Atlantic Ave
Derby Lane
Albert Meadow
Stephens Lane
The Field
Newport
Main Street
School
Ledgelawn Avenue
Glen Mary Rd
Rodick
Kennebec
High St
Roberts Ave
Cottage Street
West Street
Bridge St
Ash Place
Holland Ave
Mount Desert Street
Spring St
Bar Island Hike

3

233

3

7

Public concert in downtown Bar Harbor.

THE BEST KNOWN AND most visited town on the island, Bar Harbor serves as the unofficial headquarters of Mount Desert. The majority of the island's stores, restaurants, and hotels can be found somewhere in the vicinity of downtown Bar Harbor.

Officially incorporated in 1796 as the town of "Eden." By the 1880s the town had established itself as an international playground for the rich and famous, entertaining a steady stream of the nation's wealthiest travelers. George Vanderbilt, Joseph Pulitzer, and other titans of 19th-century industry all owned summer mansions here, while J.P. Morgan's 400-foot yacht *Corsair* often lay in the harbor.

For better or worse, by the time Eden changed its name to Bar Harbor in 1918, its glory had started to fade. In 1947 the great fire wiped out most of the multi-million dollar mansions that once lined the shore - the last remnants of what has come to be known as "The Cottage Era."

Although Bar Harbor has a drastically different face at the turn of this century than it did at the turn of the last, it still draws visitors from around the globe. A popular international cruise ship destination, each summer sees between 30 and 50 ships call to port. If you happen to be around on a day when these travelers flood the town's restaurants and shops, you might want to consider avoiding the crowds and exploring another section of the island for that particular day.

Walking Bar Harbor

Cottage, Main, Mount Desert, and West Streets constitute the majority of what there is to see and do in Bar Harbor. They are filled with clothing stores, restaurants, and more trinket shops than you can shake a Beanie Baby at. The Village Green Park is situated in the center of Bar Harbor off Main Street. Agamont Park, with excellent views of the harbor, can be found farther down Main Street towards the town pier. Locals jokingly refer to some side streets to the south of town as "Bar Harlem," but they're really just a little run down.

Walking Tour

Lasting slightly longer than an hour, this privately run tour is geared towards the history of Bar Harbor's Cottage Era. Your tour guide will be dressed as a Victorian maid or carriage driver. Filled with amusing anecdotes and rich history, this is an eye opener into Bar Harbor's fascinating past. $10 per person. June - October, 7 days a week, 8am to 8pm. 207-288-9605

❶ Shore Path

This smooth and level walk skirts the eastern shore of Bar Harbor, passes town parks, rocky beaches, and million dollar mansions. The Shore Path starts at the Town Pier at the end of Main Street, and although unmarked, it's easy to find. Just get on the asphalt sidewalk in front of the Bar Harbor Inn and head away from the shops lining Main Street. Keep in mind that much of the Shore Path is actually private property where public passage has been generously allowed. Please be respectful.

As you start the Shore Path, you'll pass the Bar Harbor Inn. Built in 1887, it was known then as the Reading Room Clubhouse. This private, all male institution was a "literary club" where most of the reading was done through the bottom of a cocktail glass. At the time Bar Harbor was a legally dry town, and the club boasted over 400 bibliophiles. Although the club shut down decades ago, the literary tradition continues. The Bar Harbor Inn's Terrace Grill serves the best Bloody Mary on the island - it comes with a giant shrimp on one side of the glass or a whole lobster claw on the other.

Continuing along the Shore Path, you'll be provided with sweeping views of Frenchman's Bay and the five Porcupine Islands. From left to right, they are Bar Island, Sheep Porcupine, Burnt Porcupine, Long Porcupine, and Bald Porcupine. Farther offshore is the white and orange lighthouse on Egg Rock Island with Schoodic Peninsula beyond.

Next you'll pass Grant Park, a public park with benches and picnic tables. There's a sign explaining the origins of the Shore Path at the southern end of the park. After passing Grant Park you'll see Balance Rock on the stony beach to your left. This striking, fifteen-foot high rock was placed here by glaciers over 13,000 years ago. Although its position looks precarious, it's actually quite secure.

The views of the harbor continue as you pass a series of privately owned mansions on your right. After crossing a small wooden bridge, the Shore Path ends at a chain link fence. At this point, you can either take a right and head over to Main Street or turn around and enjoy the Shore Path in reverse.

❷ Bar Island Hike.

One of the most unique coastal hikes in Maine. Bar Island is connected to Bar Harbor by a natural sand bar that is exposed only at low tide. Twice a day, there's a four-hour window when you can walk across the bar and explore Bar Island. A small path leads you to a lookout that has a sweeping view of Bar Harbor and the mountains beyond. Before you go, consult the local paper for a listing of the tides - to be safe you should go sometime within an hour and a half of low tide. Follow West Street away from the Bar Harbor Pier and after a few blocks take a right on Bridge Street. This will take you to the water's edge and the beginning of the sand bar. Once across, follow the trail that heads up the island. After passing a small field, the trail splits. Follow to the left and be sure to stay on the well-trodden path. This will take you to the lookout. Remember that when the tide rolls in, there's only one way back to the mainland, so keep track of the time, or plan on spending the better part of a day exploring Bar Island. One summer

a tourist parked his car on the sandbar and left it there while he kayaked around the Porcupine Islands. After several hours on the water, he returned to find the majority of his car underwater. Don't be that tourist, or you too will find yourself mentioned in future editions of this guide.

The Eccentric Joseph Pulitzer

Courtesy Bar Harbor Historical Society

B y far the strangest cottager in the history of Bar Harbor was famed newspaper mogul Joseph Pulitzer. In 1895, Pulitzer decided to spend his summers in Bar Harbor and added Chatwold to his portfolio of mansions in New York, Georgia, and

Pulitzer's cottage, Chatwold

the French Riviera. His idiosyncrasies are legendary. Pathologically sensitive to noise, the sound of a nut cracking is said to have made him wince. When Pulitzer stayed in hotels he required the rooms above, below, and on either side of him to be kept vacant. To combat the irritating noises of everyday life, Pulitzer spent $100,000 building the "Tower of Silence" on the far right of the house. This massive granite structure was specially designed to be 100% soundproof, but failed in practical use. Despite his aversion to noise, Pulitzer required a servant to read him to sleep each night and continue reading in monotone for at least two hours after he had fallen asleep - Pulitzer would wake at the slightest change in pitch.

On top of all this, Joseph Pulitzer spent at least 12 hours a day in bed. It was from this position that the mogul would often dictate letters to his secretaries in a self-devised code that contained over 20,000 names and terms. For example, Pulitzer was "Andes," Theodore Roosevelt was "glutinous," and so on. Then, in 1911 the newspaper genius who introduced the daily sports page and color comic strip passed away on his 316-foot yacht. Chatwold remained in Pulitzer's family until 1945 when it was demolished. Since 1917 his endowment has annually awarded eight coveted journalism awards.

West Street

From the town pier you can walk west on the aptly named West Street. Near the pier West Street is filled with stores and restaurants, but farther down the tree-lined street you'll catch a glimpse of some of the grand old mansions that were spared by the fire. Former Vice President Nelson Rockefeller was born on West Street in 1908. The dilapidated Bar Harbor Club, about halfway down, has been at the center of a local controversy for the better part of a decade. The owner of this prime real estate has been involved in an ongoing zoning battle with the town regarding his proposed renovations. Although this humble author makes no certain claims, I have heard rumblings from some residents that the owner is attempting to force the town into accepting his terms by letting this once grand eyesore fall into further disrepair.

Indulgences

For ice cream on a hot summer's day, look no farther than **Ben and Bill's** at the intersection of Main and Cottage Streets. They have the best ice cream on the island plus a store overflowing with gourmet chocolate treats.

If you consider yourself a culinary adventurer, try a free sample of lobster ice cream which is made with real - that's right real - lobster meat. Ben and Bill's is probably the only place in the world that makes real lobster ice cream, and there's a good reason for that. Although the onward march of Starbucks hasn't yet percolated into eastern Maine, you can still get your fix at **Benbow's Coffee Roasters**, a little farther up Main Street. And in case you were wondering, the name comes from The Admiral Benbow's, the inn at the beginning of Robert Louis Stephenson's *Treasure Island*. Continuing along Main Street, you'll come upon a black Victorian clock that has been keeping time since 1896. Across the street is **J. H. Butterfield's**, a gourmet Bar Harbor institution selling everything from smoked salmon to fine wine.

Fountain next to Agamont Park

Music and Other Diversions

Every Thursday night in season, the College of the Atlantic hosts the **Arcady Music Festival**. Performances range from the Arcady Festival Orchestra to the Maine Ragtime Festival. It's all very festive. Tickets are generally around $15. Call 207-288-3151 for more info. The **Bar Harbor Music Festival** offers weekly jazz, classical, and pops concerts in July and August. $15 Reservations recommended.207-288-5744. The **Bar Harbor Town Band** gives free evening concerts Mondays and Thursdays in July and August. Locations change but most are within earshot of Main Street. ❸ 8pm. Call the **Bar Harbor Chamber of Commerce** for more info on these and other events. 207--288-5103. A comprehensive calendar of events can be found at www.barharborinfo.com

Cinema

❹ The **Criterion Cinema** on Cottage Street is an authentic art deco movie theatre built in 1932 and listed on the National Register of Historic Places. It usually plays your standard summer Hollywood blockbusters, but half of the entertainment comes from experiencing the fabulous interior. For more

refined movies check out **Reel Pizza** on the west side of the Village Green. Reel Pizza tends to show current independent films as well as recent favorites, all from the comfort of a roomful of couches. True film buffs should arrive at the beginning of September to check out the annual **Bar Harbor Film Festival**. This week-long show-case of independent films includes screenings and lectures and usually attracts a few Hollywood notables. For more information call 207-288-3686. www.barharborfilmfest.com

Forth of July

The single busiest day of the year in Bar Harbor. For many Maine residents, Bar Harbor is the Fourth of July, and they descend upon the island in droves. The town responds with a parade, a seafood festival, outdoor concerts, and a fireworks display over the Bar Harbor Pier. For complete information contact the Bar Harbor Chamber of Commerce.

Outdoor Supplies

If you need to pick up any kind of outdoor gear check out **Cadillac Mountain Sports** at 26 Cottage Street. From wool socks to rock climbing gear, if they don't have what you need, you don't need it. **Acadia Outdoors** at 45 Main Street also offers a fairly extensive selection of supplies. **Bar Harbor Bicycle** at 48 Cottage Street offers a large selection of bikes to rent or buy. The terminally lazy can also inquire about their Cadillac Mountain Descent Trip, where they bus you to the top of the mountain and you coast down. There's also the **Bar Harbor Bicycle Shop** at 141 Cottage Street that claims the widest variety of bicycles in the state to rent or buy. Finally, **Acadia Outfitters** at 106 Cottage Street offers bike, sea kayak, and canoe rentals.

❺ St. Saviour's Episcopal Church

Built in 1877, St. Saviour's Episcopal Church is renowned for its striking collection of Tiffany stained glass windows. Located on Mount Desert Street, St. Saviour's offers free guided tours daily at 11 a.m. and 3 p.m. Even if you miss the tour, you can still step inside for a quick peek. Each summer at the turn of the century, the Vanderbilts would arrive here for Sunday services in a brass-trimmed horse drawn carriage. Then in 1915 St. Saviour's was the center of a scandal that New York gossip columnists described as the most talked about wedding of the century. It was here that the widowed bride of John Jacob Astor III - who had died three years earlier aboard the *Titanic* - gave up her multi-million dollar inheritance to marry the man she loved. Astor's will had stipulated that she must relinquish her inherited fortune if she ever remarried upon his death.

❻ Bar Harbor Historical Society

Located in the former St. Edward's Convent, the Bar Harbor Historical Society contains the definitive collection of photographs, artwork, and memorabilia from Bar Harbor's past. The collection includes historic maps and town documents, but the emphasis here is on photographs and mementos from the Cottage Era. Scrapbooks from the fire of 1947 are also on display. The Historical Society is home to virtually every book ever written about the island including many that are out of print or unavailable in stores. Worth a visit if you find yourself fascinated with Bar Harbor's opulent past. 33 Ledgelawn Avenue. Open mid-June to mid-October, 1-4pm. 207-288-0000

Bar Harbor Oceanarium

An ever popular rainy day destination, the Bar Harbor Oceanarium is filled with exhibits and information pertaining to the Maine lobster. Throughout the day the Oceanarium offers a lecture presented by a real lobsterman who will show you the tricks of the trade and answer almost any questions you might have. After checking out their collection of live specimens, you can take a stroll on the Thomas Marsh Walk. Also on the premise is a working lobster hatchery where tiny crustaceans are nurtured from birth for their eventual release into Maine waters. Here you can view young lobsters at every stage of their development and learn about the importance of the hatchery's ongoing role in maintaining healthy lobster populations. Like its counterpart in Southwest Harbor, the Bar Harbor Oceanarium boasts a consistently friendly and outstanding staff. To get there follow route 3 north of Bar Harbor. Shortly before reaching the intersection of route 3 and 102/198 you'll see a blue and white sign on your right. Open mid-May to mid-October, 9am - 5pm except Sundays. 207-288-5005

Geronimo Sculpture Garden

Exploring the funky Geronimo Sculpture Garden feels a bit like stepping through the looking glass. A windy path leads you through a small meadow filled with sculptures that look like something Dr. Seuss would make if you gave him a welder and sent him off to the dump. As the path continues,

you are led into a wooded area on the edge of a small stream. The Sculpture Garden is located on private property and is the work of a private citizen who maintains it for public enjoyment. Please be respectful. From Bar Harbor follow Route 3 until you see the Hull's Cove General Store on your left. It's located at the bottom of the hill just past the main Park entrance. Take a left on the street just before the store and follow it up the hill. About 50 yards past the General Store, you can park your car on the left side of the road. Look for the big red and white arrow that marks the start of the Garden path. Note that the path continues on the other side of the road as well. Open year round, sunrise to sunset.

7 College of the Atlantic

To the north of Bar Harbor along route 3 is the College of the Atlantic. In 1947, after the great fire devastated the island, Nelson Rockefeller commissioned a study on the economic development of the island to help rebuild the shattered communities. One of the first suggestions was the creation of a college. In 1972, with the financial backing of wealthy summer residents the College of the Atlantic was established. Heavily influenced by the social upheavals of the late sixties, its core focus centered on the study of the interrelationships between people and the environment. It offered only one major: human ecology. Today COA enrolls roughly 250 students and consistently wins the *Princeton Review*'s most-beautiful-campus award - the campus and its buildings were once part of a lavish private estate. Its students are also ranked among the happiest and best-fed in the country. Although human ecology is still the only major offered, students are exposed to a wide spectrum of liberal arts courses. www.coa.edu

Natural History Museum

Wildlife exhibits depicting the plant and animal life of coastal Maine are the highlight of the Natural History Museum. There's also a Hands-On Discovery Room where you can touch real baleen, fur, wings, and animal bones. A self-guided nature trail winds its way through the beautiful campus. Every Wednesday during the summer the Natural History Museum presents an evening lecture series. Topics change - past lectures have included Northern Ravens and the art of Edward Hopper. College of the Atlantic, Bar Harbor. Open June to mid-October. Small admission fee.

The Breakers, home of COA's Natural History Museum

The Jackson Laboratory

In 1929, ex-Harvard researcher Dr. C.C. Little founded a lab devoted to mammalian genetics and cancer research. Today the Jackson Lab is at the forefront of gene research, one of the greatest scientific revolutions in the history of mankind. Efforts at the Jackson Lab are paving the way to develop cures for diseases ranging from cancer to AIDS. One of their most important contributions is their ongoing production of JAX, a genetically unique mouse that is the researching gold standard. All told, the lab sells roughly 2 million JAX mice a year to be used at facilities around the globe. The Jackson Lab carries tremendous clout in scientific circles and is home to many of the finest researchers in the world - noted alumni include Nobel Prize winners. The Jackson Lab offers weekly lectures and films. Located on the outskirts of Bar Harbor. Follow Route 3 towards Seal Harbor and look for a red brick building on your left. www.jax.org 207-288-6000

Mount Desert Island Biological Laboratory

Founded in 1898, the MDI Biological Laboratory is devoted to the education and research of marine organisms to promote human health. Originally conceived as a teaching institution, the emphasis later shifted to research. The lab is a world leader in electrolyte and transport physiology. Free visitors' tours are offered once a week in the summer. Call 207-288-3605 for the latest times. www.mdibl.org

Compass Harbor

This easy one-mile walk passes by the remains of the estate of George Dorr on its way to the quiet pebble beaches of Compass Harbor. The walk starts next to an unmarked parking area exactly one mile south of the intersection of Main and Mount Desert Streets in downtown Bar Harbor. The gravel parking area is on your left - if you reach the Ocean Drive Motor Court, you've gone too far. Follow the old road heading east to get to Compass Harbor.

Bar Harbor Whale Museum

Home to a full-sized skeleton of a minke whale. Dolphin and Seal skeletons are also on display and films on marine mammals are shown throughout the day. And you can't beat the price: free. Bar Harbor, 52 West Street.

The Cat

This high-speed ferry rockets cars and passengers to Yarmouth, Nova Scotia, in a little under 3 hours. While cruising through international waters, you can try to win back your fare at the ferry's onboard casino that includes slot machines, blackjack, and roulette. Before the 55mph *Cat* came on the scene, the much slower *Blue Nose Ferry* shuttled visitors to Nova Scotia. When *The Cat* was first introduced, its enormous wake was the subject of a maritime controversy that ultimately forced it to lower its departure speed until it reaches open water. But some resistance to the new ferry still lingers, earning it the less than endearing nickname "*The Rat.*" Travel packages are available.1-888-249-7245. www.nfl-bay.com

Driving Tours

These narrated tours start in Bar Harbor and continue along the Park Loop Road. If you're a big fan of narrated tours, go for it, otherwise drive the Park Loop Road yourself and keep your own clock. **Oli's Trolley** offers open air trolley tours. 62 Main Street, 207-288-9899. **Acadia National Park Tours**, offers both bus and trolley tours. 53 Main Street. 207-288-3327

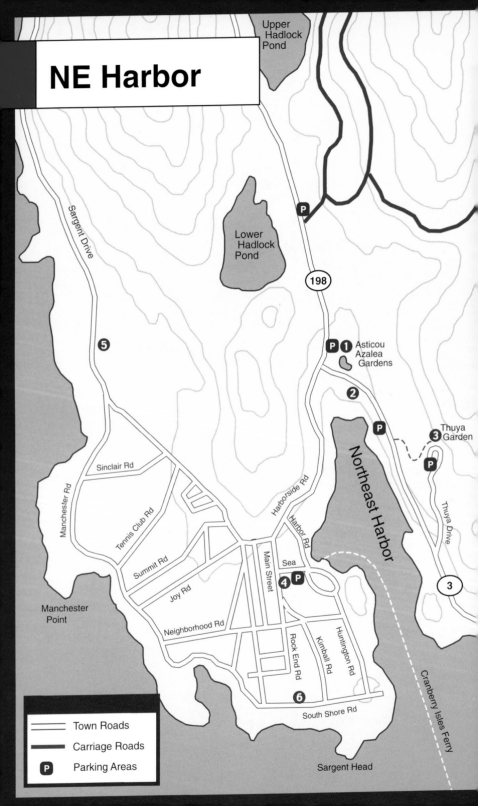

Spring painting off Northeast Harbor

ISLAND PUBLICATIONS SOMETIMES describe Northeast Harbor as a "Sailing Community." Just like Beverly Hills is a "Shopping Community." Although sailing is quite popular here, the town is much more renowned for its sense of affluence and concentration of multi-million dollar summer homes.

At the turn of the century when Bar Harbor began to suffer from overdevelopment, wealthy visitors started buying property here. Eventually the emphasis shifted and Northeast Harbor claimed its title as the place to be on Mount Desert. Its exclusive lifestyle commands some of the highest real estate values on the island, a distinction it shares with neighboring Seal Harbor. Some houses in Northeast Harbor have rented for upwards of $40,000 a month. Not surprisingly, some locals in other towns like to joke about the NERKs (NorthEast Rich Kids) that show up each summer.

The town's deep, sheltered harbor is considered one of the finest along the coast of Maine, and during the summer it's filled with fabulous yachts. But don't fret if yours isn't one of them. The town still offers plenty of inexpensive activities for you to take advantage of.

Although Northeast Harbor is on the southeast side of the island, it gets its name from being northeast of Southwest Harbor, which is southwest of Bar Harbor, to the northeast.

Asticou Azalea Garden

❶ Asticou Azalea Garden

Each spring over 50 varieties of azaleas, rhododendrons, and laurels explode in a full bloom of color at the Asticou Azalea Garden. Many of these plants were transplanted from Reef Point - the garden of famed Bar Harbor landscape architect Beatrix Farrand. Even if you miss the blossoms, the garden is still worth a visit. Its carefully manicured grounds make it a favorite location for wedding photographers. There's also a distinct Asian influence that culminates in a Zen rock garden. The Asticou Azalea Garden is located across the street from the Asticou Inn. There's a small parking lot on Route 198 a short way up from the junction with Route 3. Follow the carefully laid out sand path that starts at the southern end of the parking lot. Open sunrise to sunset, May through October.

❷ Asticou Inn

One of the most famous landmarks on Mount Desert, this fifty-room inn is located off route 3 overlooking Northeast Harbor. Named after the Wabanaki chief who lured a group of French Settlers to the island nearly four centuries ago, the building was designed by noted island architect Fred Savage. When celebrities visit Mount Desert, they often wind up staying here. 207-276-3344

❸ Thuya Garden

Located on a hill overlooking Northeast Harbor, Thuya Garden is without a doubt the nicest public garden on the island. The grounds are part of a land trust that was set up by Joseph Curtis, a Boston Landscape architect who summered in the adjacent cottage. The cottage is now open to the public and contains an extensive collection of botanical literature. Interestingly enough, Curtis never set eyes on the garden. It was laid out in 1953 by Charles K. Savage, the first administrator of the Asticou Terraces Trust. The name comes from *Thuja occidentalis*, the American white cedar found throughout the area. A pair of thick wooden gates decorated with carvings of plants and animals guard the entrance to the garden. There are two ways to get to Thuya Garden; up a small trail by foot or up a small road by car. Unless you or a person with you is handicapped, take the trail - it's worth it.

By foot - from the junction of Route 3/198 drive about a half-mile southeast on Route three until you reach the "Asticou Terraces" parking lot on your right. If the road opens up to great views of Northeast Harbor, you've gone too far. The path starts on the stone walkway across the road from the parking lot. The path splits in several places, but all routes ultimately lead to the garden. Along the way you'll be treated to elevated views of Northeast Harbor.

By car - continue past the Thuya parking lot and take your first left up Thuya Drive. Follow the road up the hill until you reach the cul-de-sac at the end. Thuya Garden is open from July through September, 7am to 7pm.

Thuya Garden

Afternoon boating in Northeast Harbor

❹ Great Harbor Maritime Museum

Devoted to the history and culture of boating on Mount Desert, the Great Harbor Museum boasts a small, but growing, collection. Sailing photographs, small boats, and historic nautical equipment all find a home here. Seasonal exhibits range from sailboat racing to lobstering. Arts and educational programs are offered during the summer. FYI - Great Harbor refers to the general area of Northeast Harbor, Southwest Harbor, and the Cranberry Isles. 207-276-5262. Northeast Harbor, Old Fire House on Main Street. Open seasonally, Mon - Sat, 10am-5pm. Small adimission fee.

High End Shopping

Not surprisingly, Northeast Harbor is home to some of the finest shopping on the island, and it is home to the best art galleries on Mount Desert. All can be found on the two-block stretch of Main Street that constitutes downtown Northeast Harbor. **Samuel Shaw Contemporary Jewelry**, 100 Main Street, offers distinctive jewelry and artwork. A graduate of the Rhode Island School of Design, Shaw has been creating bracelets, necklaces, earrings, and other forms of jewelry out of pebbles from Maine beaches for years. The gallery also features works by other craftsmen. **Northeast Harbor Art & Antiques** offers antique furniture, artwork, and maritime equipment including brass telescopes and lanterns - perfect for old salts with a few dubloons to spare. Located off the intersection of Three Summit Road and Main Street.

➎ Sargent Drive

Finally, where Northeast Harbor borders Somes Sound, you'll find Sargent Drive. This small stretch of road winds past several spectacular mansions before opening up to some fantastic views of Somes Sound - the only natural fjord in the eastern United States. Stories exist that in the 1600s the British navy once chased a fleeing pirate into the sound. After patiently waiting for him at the entrance, they sailed in to discover that both the pirate and his ship had disappeared without a trace. Later on, the British soldiers overheard a group of local natives speaking of an underwater cave in Somes Sound that leads to an above ground opening in the woods. Pressed for an explanation, they concluded that the pirate had hidden his treasure in the cave, scuttled his ship, and escaped over the land. Neither the treasure nor the cave was ever found.

➏ Petite Plaisance

Each summer hundreds of international scholars come to Northeast Harbor to visit one house. Petite Plaisance was the permanent home of French novelist Marguerite Yourcenar, whose 1951 novel *Memoirs of Hadrian* launched her into international literary fame. She was the first woman inducted as an "immortal" into the Academie Francaise, founded in 1635 and comprised of no more than forty members at any one time. Yourcenar moved to Northeast Harbor from France after the outbreak of World War II. Once here she decided that she could never live anywhere else. French journalists disliked her U.S. residency and often referred to her as a recluse. Before she died in 1987, she set up a trust to ensure that Petite Plaisance would be open to guests in perpetuity. "Madame always liked to have the last word," claims one of the curators. Petite Plaisance is open from June 15 to August 31 by appointment only. Call 207-276-3940 for more information.

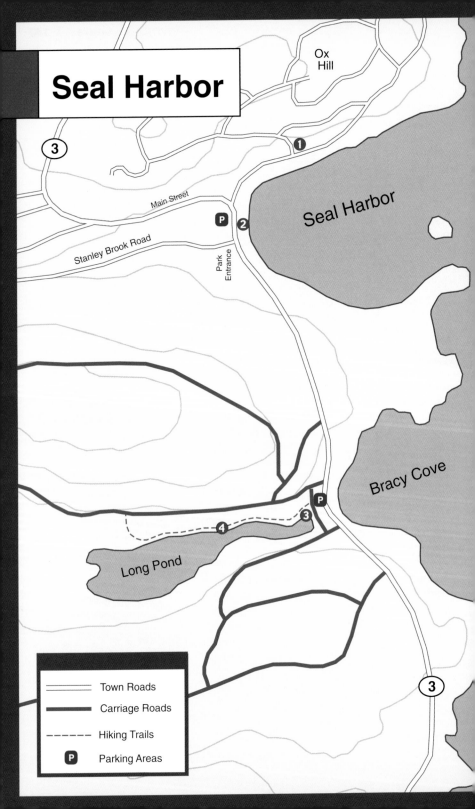

Seal Harbor from a private residence on Ox Hill

IF NORTHEAST HARBOR IS RENOWNED as *the* wealthy summer community of the island, Seal Harbor is known for its quiet affluence, and its inhabitants would prefer to keep it that way. In the early part of the century, the Astors, Fords, and Rockefellers all owned cottages in Seal Harbor. Today many of their descendants reside in the hills overlooking the bay. Hardly concerned with securing their social status, they came here to escape the clutter of Bar Harbor and enjoy the quiet pleasures of pastoral island life. John D. Rockefeller, Jr. exemplified this lifestyle, avoiding showy dinner parties and preferring to spend his time chopping wood. This attitude is as true today as it was back then, which accounts for the noticeable lack of any commercial development.

At one point Seal Harbor was a bit of a vacation destination. The Seaside Inn, a grand Queen Ann-style summer hotel, was once located across the beach on the site of the present-day Park entrance. The inn featured a 150-foot long veranda from which guests could relax and take in the views. But Seal Harbor residents like their privacy. In 1963 the Rockefeller family purchased the Seaside Inn and promptly had it demolished. Although hardly a tourist attraction, there are still a few worthy treasures in the area that can be enjoyed by all.

In 1910 President Taft visited Mount Desert on vacation and sailed his yacht into Seal Harbor. As his boat approached the shore, a crowd of onlookers gathered by the town dock. When Taft disembarked from his boat and stepped onto the dock, his 300-pound frame started to tip it over. A swarm of greeters instantly rushed to his aid. While they managed to save the poor President from falling in, their combined weight forced the dock partially underwater. Such marked President Taft's soggy introduction to Mount Desert Island.

❶ Seal Harbor Library

If you continue straight on the road, you'll come upon the Seal Harbor Public Library located in a small, white building. This quaint jewel is only open a few hours each week, but a quick glimpse inside will speak volumes about the elegant simplicity of life in Seal Harbor.

Ox Hill

Facing the ocean from the beach, you'll notice Ox Hill on your left. This is where the majority of Seal Harbor's multi-million dollar estates are located. Cottages with names like Felsmere, Keewaydin, and Glengariff reside here. Even Martha Stewart's own Skylands calls Ox Hill home. Many of these houses were designed by New York architect Duncan Candler, a graduate of Paris' famed Ecole des Beaux-Arts. A trademark of Candler's architecture in Seal Harbor is his signature pergola, a wooden arbor covered with vegetation.

❷ Seal Harbor Town Beach

Across from the Village Green you'll see the Seal Harbor Beach. This is one of two natural sand beaches on the island - the other being Sand Beach off the Park Loop Road. On sunny days this beach can be a good alternative to the swarms of visitors found at other swimming holes. The shallow water even reaches somewhat bearable temperatures on hot summer days.

Skylands

Courtesy Maine Historic Preservation Commission

When Henry Ford's son Edsel decided he needed a summer home in 1922, he set his sights on Seal Harbor. Edsel purchased 80 wooded acres on Ox Hill and commissioned architect Duncan Candler to design a palatial estate. When completed in 1925, Skylands included a main house, a guesthouse, a play house, a squash court, a tennis court, extensive gardens, and a garage and stable. Set into the hillside, the name came from the stunning views the location commanded.

In 1997, the estate's fame was forever ensured when it was purchased by the doyenne of domesticity, Martha Stewart. Since her arrival, Martha has become the distinguished neighbor that many local residents love to hate. It seems like every summer a new rumor involving Martha's bad behavior spreads like wildfire around the island. Although there could be a grain of truth to some of the stories, most people close to the situations admit they are wildly off base. Whatever the case, pictures of Skylands' decadent interior are often featured in Martha's magazines and on her syndicated television show.

❸ Little Long Pond

Want to live like a Rockefeller? Continue along windy route 3 until you come upon Little Long Pond on your left. While the lands surrounding the pond are owned by the Rockefeller family, they have generously been left open to public use. Although Carriage Roads pass through the property, here they are open only to horses and pedestrians - no bikes. Follow the path to ❹ the right of the pond until you reach the **Rockefeller boathouse**. This beautiful building is still used to house the family's old-fashioned wooden boats. If you think the water looks inviting, think again. Leeches are quite fond of Little Long Pond.

The hill behind the boathouse was once the site of the Eyrie, John D. Rockefeller, Jr.'s 100-room plus cottage. After an addition designed by Duncan Candler, the Eyrie contained over twenty bathrooms, twenty fireplaces, and two elevators. At that time the lands of Rockefeller's estate covered over a thousand acres and stretched all the way back to Jordan Pond. Sadly, the Eyrie was torn down in 1963 after Rockefeller's death.

❶ Mount Desert Historical Society

Housed in the white building near the arched bridge. The Historical Society contains photographs and artifacts, and inside you can purchase a small historical guide and walking tour of Somesville. The most prominent feature of the town is the footbridge next to the Historical Society, one of the most photographed landmarks on the island. The small building to the left is the Selectman's Office, which was used at various times as a cobbler's shop, post office, and school. The footbridge was built to commemorate a descendant of the Somes family, the island's first settlers.

❷ Of Interest

Bookstore lovers will not want to pass up a visit to **Port in a Storm**. Located on the water overlooking Somes Sound, it sports one of the widest selections of books on Mount Desert. The *Maine Times* reader's survey consistently ranks it as the best bookstore in Maine. Open Mon-Sat 9:30-5:30, ❸ Sun 1-5. 207-244-4114 acadia.net/portbks. Also of note is the **Acadia Repertory Theatre**, located in the old Masonic Hall. From early July to mid-September the theatre puts on live performances of classic plays, including an annual Agatha Christie murder mystery. Special children's programs are offered on Wednesday and Saturday mornings, and regular performances happen every night of the week except Monday. 207-244-7260

Seal Cove Auto Museum

Seal Cove Auto Museum

Seal Cove summer resident Richard Paine, Jr. began restoring autos as a boy, and today his collection contains over 100 antique cars and motorcycles. Rolls Royces, Packards, and Chadwicks are just some of the classic autos on display. This is truly a world-class collection. Even the sparse warehouse setting can't take away from the cars' grandeur. To get there take a right just south of Somesville onto Route 102 and keep your eyes open for museum signs. The building is at the end of a long driveway on your right. Open June through mid-September, 10am to 5pm. Small admission fee.

Pretty Marsh

If you've already headed over to the Seal Cove Auto Museum, continue along Route 102 to visit Pretty Marsh. This quiet and secluded spot is located right on the water and is a perfect location for an afternoon lunch. There's a small wooden porch with picnic tables overlooking the water. Following Route 102 past the Seal Cove Auto Museum, keep your eyes out for signs that will direct you to a road on your right that brings you to Pretty Marsh.

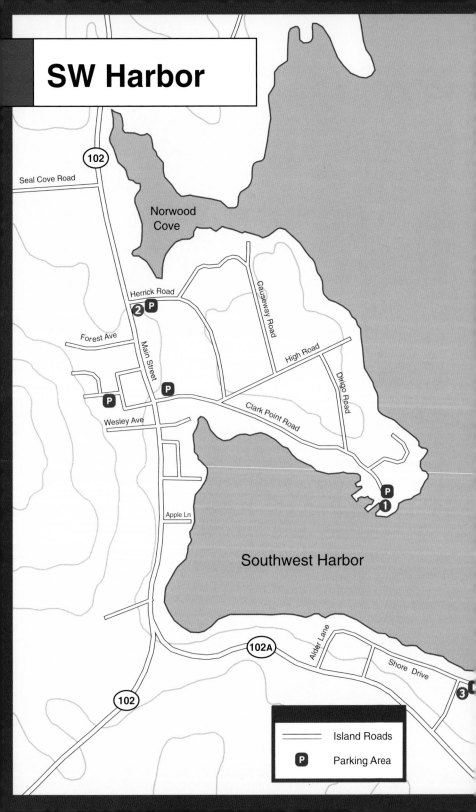

Pier off Southwest Harbor

HOME TO BOATBUILDERS, FISHERMEN, and summer residents who cherish the "quiet side" of Mount Desert, Southwest Harbor can be the perfect anecdote to Bar Harbor during peak tourist season. It offers similar stores, restaurants, and museums on a much smaller scale in a much less visited town. Although Main Street in Southwest Harbor caters to the tourist trade, it is also ranked as one of the top ten commercial fishing harbors in Maine.

During the mid-1800s Southwest Harbor was at the center of life on Mount Desert. It was the island's main commercial hub and the only place steamships would call to port. For a brief time hotel development flourished as the town braced itself for the coming boom. However, numerous personal accounts from that era describe in no small detail the putrid smell of Southwest Harbor's fish canneries. Some historians have speculated that this terrible odor was partly responsible for the tourist migration towards the eastern side of the island. Whatever the case, the last cannery closed its doors years ago and the town smells great.

Festivals

Southwest Harbor is home to a few notable summer celebrations. The Quiet Side Festival usually happens in June and offers food, music, and boat races. Then in October, over twenty Maine microbrewers descend on the town for its annual Oktoberfest celebration. Beer, food, music, and beer are the highlights of this event. Kayak festivals and garden tours also take place in Southwest Harbor. For dates, locations, and complete information, contact the Chamber of Commerce. 207-244-9264

❶ Oceanarium

Did you know that sea scallops have up to 150 eyes? Or that starfish can see out of the tips of their legs? You would if you visited the Oceanarium in Southwest Harbor. Live scallops and starfish are just two of the sea creatures on display at this fascinating - if not slightly dilapidated - facility. Here you can listen to the song of a humpback whale and learn about fishing techniques on Mount Desert. There's also a saltwater touch tank with starfish, horseshoe crabs, and sea cucumbers. Located at the end of Clark Point Road. Open mid-May to mid-October, 9am to 5pm except Sundays. Small admission fee. 207-244-7330

Private residence overlooking Southwest Harbor

Birdcarving workshop at the Wendell Gilley Museum

② Wendell Gilley Museum

Wendell Gilley was a Southwest Harbor resident who took up wooden bird carving as a hobby and was eventually honored as one of the country's finest folk artists. The museum displays his life's work of over 200 hand carved birds. A short film is frequently shown that provides a terrific glimpse into both Gilley's life and life growing up on Mount Desert. Exhibits feature other noted wildlife artists, and woodcarving demonstrations are often given during the day. The museum is also the unofficial bird-lover headquarters of the island. Its gift shop offers books, binoculars, and a knowledgeable staff. Small admission fee. Open June - Christmas, Summer hours Tues - Sun, 10am - 4pm. Small admission fee. 207-244-7555 www.acadia.net/gilley

The Claremont Hotel

Listed on the National Register of Historic Places, the Claremont offers one of the finest views of Somes Sound on the island. Even if you're not a guest, you can still enjoy them from the Claremont's dining room where breakfast and dinner are served. They also offer lunch from their waterfront boat-house in July and August. The Claremont also hosts an annual croquet tournament on their grounds at the beginning of August. 207-244-5036. www.acadia.net/claremont

Bass Harbor Lighthouse

❶ Bass Harbor Lighthouse

Located on the southernmost tip of the island, the Bass Harbor Lighthouse has been guiding mariners since 1858. Often romanticized, the life of a lighthouse keeper was a difficult and lonely one. Today nearly every lighthouse on the coast is fully automated, including this one. The property is still maintained by the U.S. Coast Guard and high-ranking officials have the option to live here.

❷ Wonderland

A mile and a half east of the lighthouse on Route 102 is Wonderland, an easily accessible stretch of classic Maine coastline. An abandoned roadway leads you through the woods to peaceful cobblestone beaches and tidal pools. Wonderland graces the shore of Bennet Harbor. The Duck Islands are visible to the southeast and Great Cranberry Island lies to the northeast.

❸ Ship Harbor Nature Trail

Located between Wonderland and the Bass Harbor Lighthouse, the Ship Harbor Nature Trail is a short circular loop that skirts the ocean and reveals some fantastic hidden spots. Like Wonderland, the Nature Trail is overlooked by most visitors, so crowds are rarely a problem. In 1739, an Irish Schooner filled with wealthy passengers was driven off course and crashed at Ship Harbor. At the time Mount Desert did not have a permanent European settlement, and the passengers found themselves trapped on a deserted island. When a rescue ship finally arrived in the dead of winter, it found only a handful of survivors, shivering in yards of expensive Irish linen.

offshore islands

Cranberry Isles

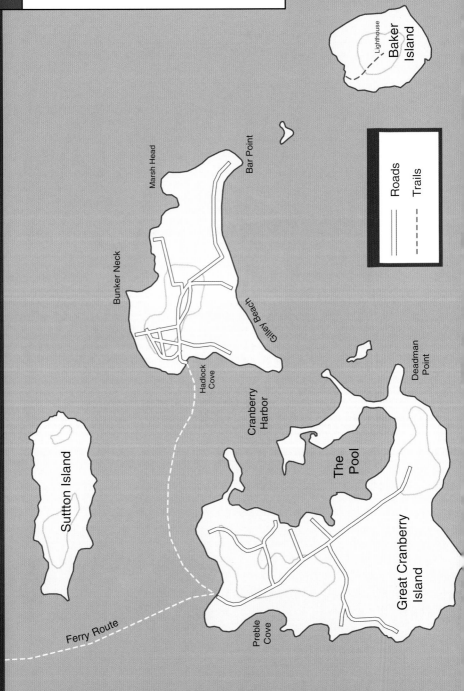

Baker Island

Lighthouse

Roads

Trails

Marsh Head

Bar Point

Bunker Neck

Gilley Beach

Hadlock Cove

Cranberry Harbor

Deadman Point

The Pool

Suttton Island

Great Cranberry Island

Preble Cove

Ferry Route

Cranberry Isles

LYING JUST TWO MILES away from the southeastern shores of Mount Desert, the Cranberry Isles are genuine coastal islands where lobstering and fishing are still the dominant occupations. Originally named for the bogs that provided early American sailors with vitamin C-rich cranberries that helped prevent scurvy, today you will be hard pressed to find any free samples of this delicious fruit. The bogs were drained decades ago in a somewhat successful attempt to control mosquito populations. The Cranberry Isles were home to some of the earliest permanent settlements in the region. Not only were they easily defended but the small islands were also a perfect choice for raising livestock - no fencing was needed since the animals could never stray too far.

You can explore either Great Cranberry or Little Cranberry Island on foot, but if you have a bike, it makes getting around that much easier. If time is an issue and you only want to visit one island, make it Little Cranberry which offers nearly identical scenery to Great Cranberry plus a museum and a restaurant located right on the water.

Getting to the Cranberry Isles

The most popular method of transportation is the Beal & Bunker Mailboat. They deliver mail year-round but Beal & Bunker also doubles as a water shuttle, ferrying people to and from the Cranberry Isles throughout the day. From mid-June through Labor Day, they'll take you to Great Cranberry, Islesford, and back for $10, $5 for kids under 12. Bike transportation is an extra $2. The first trip leaves Northeast Harbor at 7:30am and the last trip from Islesford leaves at 6:30pm. On Sundays the first trip leaves at 10am. Off-season schedules are a bit different. Call for exact departure times (207-244-3575) or pick up a free copy of their ferry schedule at the Northeast Harbor town pier. The Cranberry Cove Boating Company departs from Southwest Harbor and offers comparable schedules and rates. 207-244-5882. The Islesford Ferry Co. offers a four-and-a-half hour nature trip to Baker Island, part of Acadia National Park. In July and August a park naturalist accompanies the cruise that culminates in a hike on Baker Island. $16 adults, $11 children. 207-276-3717

Great Cranberry Island

The largest of the Cranberry Islands, Great Cranberry's roads offer the most extensive biking . As you explore the roads, chances are good that you might catch a glimpse of the deer that freely roam the island. For decades deer hunting has been banned on the Cranberry Isles, but residents have recently become so fed up with the pesky creatures feeding on their gardens that they voted to repeal the ban. Also keep your eyes peeled for some of the carefully balanced rock sculptures found throughout the island. These gravity defying creations often line the roads or are hidden in the nearby woods and are the work of local island artists. **The Red House** offers overnight accommodations from Memorial to Columbus Day. Rooms in this 18th-century cottage run from $60-80 a night. Reservations are essential. 207-244-5297. Shopping consists of the **Great Cranberry General Store** which offers basic supplies near the pier and the **Whale's Rib** Gift Shop halfway down the main road.

Islesford (Little Cranberry Island)

Just off the dock where you'll be dropped off, the **Islesford Dock Restaurant** serves fresh seafood from one of the most spectacular vantage points in the region. They offer both lunch and dinner (reservations recommended for dinner) and Sunday brunch. Boaters should note that they also rent moorings for overnight stays. 207-244-7494. In the red brick building to the left of the town dock, you'll find the **Islesford Historical Museum**. The museum is devoted to the cultural and maritime history of the Cranberry Isles. Photographs, antique furniture, and other memorabilia are all on display here. Open daily from 10:45am to 4:30pm, mid-June to Labor Day. **Islesford Artists** is a gallery showcasing the work of local artisans and is located a bit down the main road. 207-244-3145

Great Cranberry town pier

Sutton Island

Sutton Island consists of privately owned land. The mail boat might stop here en route to Great Cranberry but unless you or somebody you know owns a home here, don't plan on getting off. In 1755 Ebenezer Sutton purchased this island from the local Wabanakis for two quarts of rum, half what his friend Abraham Somes paid for nearby Greenings Island. Thirty years later land was offered at the price of five Spanish Milled Dollars for 100 acres. Real estate values have gone up sharply since then.

Baker Island

Owned by Acadia National Park, Baker Island is a natural land preserve with a short hiking trail and spectacular views of Mount Desert. In the 1800s the 12 person Gilley family lived alone on Baker's Island and operated a small saltwater farm. They lived almost entirely on natural resources - fishing, farming, and making clothes out of home grown wool. Still, each Sunday the family traveled seven miles in an open boat to attend the Congregational Church in Southwest Harbor.

The best kept secret in the region

❺ Fine Sand Beach

Off the beaten path is definitely one way to describe the location of this beach, but no one who gets here ever regrets making the journey. The sugary, white sand combines with shallow water and fantastic views to make this the nicest beach in mid-coast Maine. To get there from the Atlantic Blanket company, continue on the road and take your next left onto a rough, dirt road. Continue on for 3/4 of a mile making sure to bear right past the fork in the road. There's a small grove where you can park at the bottom of the hill on the left. A path starts at the parking area that leads you on a short hike through the woods to the beach.

❻ Quarry Pond

Located at the top of a hill overlooking the harbor, this abandoned rock quarry offers roped-off freshwater swimming. There's even a dock in the middle where you can catch a few rays. To get there, follow the road that passes along the eastern side of Burnt Coat Harbor. As the road starts to loop around near the southern tip, look for a dirt road heading uphill on the right that will take you to Quarry Pond.

outdoor adventures

Kayaking

Coastal
Mount Desert's towering mountains, rugged coastline, and high concentration of small offshore islands makes it one of the top coastal kayaking spots in the country. Somes Sound and the area around the Porcupine Islands are two of the most popular daytime routes, while the northwest tip of the island makes for a spectacular sunset paddle. If you didn't bring your own kayak, there are several stores in Bar Harbor that will rent you one or take you on a guided tour. The latter is nice because they deal with the hassle of transportation - all you have to do is paddle.

Freshwater
All lakes and ponds on Mount Desert are open to canoeing and kayaking. The most popular places to do so are Long Pond, Jordan Pond, and Eagle Lake. There are usually boat launches close to parking areas at each.

The following vendors all offer Kayak rentals and guided tours
- **Acadia Bike and Canoe**, 48 Cottage St., Bar Harbor 288-9605
- **Acadia Outfitters**, 106 Cottage St., Bar Harbor 288-8118
- **Island Adventures Sea Kayaking**, 137 Cottage St, Bar Harbor 288-3886
- **Loon Bay Kayak**, Southwest Harbor, 266-8888
- **National Park Kayaking**, 39 Cottage St., Bar Harbor 288-0342

Preparing to paddle around the Porcupine Islands

Swimming

There's nothing more exhilarating this side of the arctic than a dip in the ocean at Sand Beach. But for those unwilling to brave the icy waters off Mount Desert, a more suitable alternative exists. There are several freshwater lakes and ponds throughout the island where swimming is permitted, and you can cool off without going numb. Although often tempting, swimming is prohibited at Eagle Lake, Jordan Pond, Upper and Lower Hadlock Pond, and the southern tip of Long Pond since they are all public water supplies. Yes, you can be fined. But other than those five spots, you can swim anywhere you want. Listed below are some of the best locations.

Echo Lake Beach
Probably the most popular swimming hole. Echo Lake can still be a bit cold in June, but as the summer progresses, it starts to warm up. By August temperatures range from perfect to perfect. Echo Lake Beach at the southern shore is a man-made beach with dramatic views of the rock cliffs that tower above. There's a lifeguard on duty which makes it popular among families with young children. A busy spot throughout the summer, be forewarned that crowds can sometimes become unbearable on weekends in July and August. To get to the beach follow 102 heading south from Somesville towards Southwest Harbor. As you drive, you'll catch a glimpse of the northern half of Echo Lake on your right. Take a right where you see a brown sign that says "Acadia National Park" and follow the road to the end. The beach is at the bottom of the stairs near the end of the parking lot.

Echo Lake Ledges
The ledges are a rock outcropping that contains sections elevated about two feet above the water. If you do jump into the water be aware that the water is shallow here. There's a parking lot next to the ledges on 102 before you reach the turnoff for Echo Beach. You'll see a brown sign for parking at Acadia Mountain, and the parking lot is on your right. In the middle of the parking lot, a set of stairs leads you on a short path through the woods that ends at the water's edge.

Lake Wood

During the early summer when other lakes are filled with melted snow, Lake Wood's shallow waters prove remarkably swimable. The downside comes later in the summer when bathtub-like conditions can arise. From Bar Harbor follow Route 3 until you reach Hulls Cove. Take a left on the Crooked Road and follow it for 3/4 of a mile, at which point you'll take another left on unpaved Park Road. At the end of the road, there's a small parking area with a path that leads to a pebble beach. A small trail to the left leads you to a flat rock outcropping that you can lie down on or jump off - the exposed iron bolts were part of an old diving board. The water here is over 6 feet deep.

Long Pond Beach

Long Pond is the largest body of water on Mount Desert, over four miles long from tip to tip. Although in places Long Pond is over 100 feet deep, Jordan Pond - at 150 feet - still remains the deepest. At the northern tip of Long Pond is a small beach with a gentle grade, perfect for small children. To get there from Somesville, take a right on 102 towards Pretty Marsh. Follow 102 for a mile and a half until you see the beach on your left.

Long Pond Cliffs - Duck Rock

Although swimming is prohibited at the southern tip of Long Pond, from Duck Rock north everything is kosher. A short hike can take you from the southern tip to the top of Duck Rock. From here you have two options: you can follow the small, steep path on the right down to the water's edge and slide quietly into the water, or you can let out a yelp and jump from the top of Duck Rock into the deep water below. If you do take the plunge, be sure to jump out and away from the rock - the goal here is to hit the water. I have never in all my years heard of anyone injuring themselves on Duck Rock. But there is always a person out there who can hurt themselves on anything, so I must state for the record that I take no responsibility for any injuries you may suffer from jumping off the top of the rock.

To get to Duck Rock from Southwest Harbor, follow 102 north and take a left on Seal Cove Road just outside of downtown. After about three quarters of a mile, take a right on Long Pond Road and follow it to the end. You'll come upon a water pumping station and a small parking lot. Park your car and follow the path on the right that hugs the shoreline. Eventually you'll pass by two private houses. Right after passing the second one, follow the path that veers towards the pond. You'll climb up a small hill and soon wind up at a small clearing that marks the top of Duck Rock.

Summer daredevil Chris Tannis performs
a Triple Lindy off Duck Rock.

Power Boat Cruises

No matter how much time you've spent *on* Mount Desert, you have never really seen the island until you've seen it from the water. The view is simply amazing. If you do head out on the water, remember sunglasses, sunblock, and warm clothes. Even on hot days it can get chilly on the open ocean.

Sea Princess
> Departs Northeast Harbor - 207-276-5352
> - Somes Sound cruise. 1.5 hrs. $12, children $8
> - Cranberry Island cruise. 2.75 hrs. $15, children $10
> - Sunset dinner cruise. 3 hrs. $12, children $8

Water Lilly
> Departs Southwest Harbor - 207-244-7927
> - Somes Sound cruise. 2 hrs. $20 / person
> - Cranberry Island cruise. 2 hrs. $13 / person
> - Private charters available

Islesford Ferry
> Departs Northeast Harbor - 207-276-3717
> - Nature and Island Lunch Cruise.
>   2.5 hrs. Trip to Little Cranberry Island. $13, children under 12 $7
> - Baker Island Cruise.
>   4.5 hrs. Trip to Baker Island led by Acadia National Park naturalist. Hike included. $18, children $10.

Katherine
> Departs Bar Harbor - 207-288-3322
> - Working lobster boat hauls real lobster traps to show to passengers. Harbor seal watching also included. 1.5 hrs.

The Cat
> Departs Bar Harbor - 1-888-249-7245
> - Ferry Service to Yarmouth, Nova Scotia. 2.75 hrs.

Acadian
>Departs Bar Harbor - 207-288-3322
>• Nature tour of porpoises, seals, and marine birds. 2 hrs.

Sunrise
>Departs Northeast Harbor - 207-276-5352
>• Lobster tour of Somes Sound. Lobster traps are hauled and each person gets their own fresh, cooked lobster. 2.5 hrs.

Whale Watching

The most popular boating excursions. Whale watches generally last from two to four hours, travel about 25 miles offshore, and are one of the most comfortable ways to get out on the water. Most trips see humpback, finback, and minke whales. Although there is always the possibility that you might not see a single whale, all of the companies listed below offer cash back guarantees.

>Bar Harbor Whale Watch Company, *Friendship V,* 112 ft. catamaran
>Departs Bar Harbor - 1-800-WHALES-4
>• Whale watch & puffin cruises

>Whale Watcher Inc., *Atlantis ,* 116 ft.
>Departs Bar Harbor - 207-288-3322
>• Whale watch, puffin, seal, & seabird trips
>• Park ranger cruise
>• VIP estate cruise
>• Sunset nature cruise

>Acadian Whale Watch Company, *Acadian Whale Watcher*
>Departs Bar Harbor - 1-800-247-3794
>• Whale watch & puffin cruises
>• Sunset whale watching
>• Lighthouse/nature cruise

Sailing Cruises

One of the most relaxing ways to get out on the water. Although you won't be able to cover as much ground as you would on a powerboat, there is nothing that compares to the laid-back, peaceful experience of letting the wind carry you around the island.

Blackjack Sail Boat Charters, *Blackjack,* 33 ft. Friendship Sloop
Departs Northeast Harbor - 207-244-7813
Cruises of the Cranberry Isles

Downeast Windjammer Cruises, *Margaret Todd,* 151 ft. four-masted schooner
Departs Bar Harbor - 207-288-4585
2 hour Windjammer cruises
$25 / person

Rachel B. Jackson, *Rachel B. Jackson,* 67 ft. wooden schooner
Departs Southwest Harbor - 207-244-7813
Tours of Somes Sound and Great Harbor.
Adults $22, Children $14

Scenic Flights

The towering mountains and sheer cliffs of Mount Desert are an impressive sight from the air. **Acadia Air**, next to the Bar Harbor Airport in Trenton offers scenic flights from $17/ person and up. They offer several routes ranging in time from ten to forty minutes. Their best route is the Somes Sound trip ($25) that flies over the dramatic eastern half of Mount Desert and then circles back up Somes Sound. Choose a clear, sunny day to go since coastal fog and haze drastically cut down on visibility. 207-667-5534

Bird Watching

Mount Desert is home to over 300 species of birds. One of the best bird watching areas is at the Sieur de Monts Visitor Center off the Park Loop Road. For full- and half-day nature tours call **Downeast Nature Tours**: 207-288-8128. The Sea Bird Watcher Co. offers boat cruises geared towards sea bird viewing. 207-288-5033.

Fishing

Freshwater Fishing
Fishing is allowed on all lakes and ponds on Mount Desert although fishing at the Tarn - just south of Bar Harbor - is restricted to senior citizens and children under 16. You'll have to obtain a permit for all freshwater fishing, available at sporting good stores, hardware stores, and town offices throughout the island.

Ocean Fishing
No permit is required for ocean fishing. If you don't have a sea-worthy vessel, you can purchase a ticket aboard the M/V *Seal*. $35 for a four-hour journey. Trips depart from the Bar Harbor Inn Pier. 207-288-4585.

Golf

Kebo Valley Club
Bar Harbor. 18 holes, par 70. 207-288-3000

Northeast Harbor Golf Club
18 holes, par 69. 207-276-5335

Causeway Club
Southwest Harbor. 18 holes, par 65. 207-244-3780

the
lobster
bible

FOR MANY PEOPLE summers on Mount Desert and fresh cooked lobster are one and the same. I am thoroughly convinced that a moist piece of lobster meat drenched in melted butter is God's gift to Maine. Even if you are only here for a weekend, no visit to MDI is complete without at least one lobster dinner. For that reason this section has been included as a complete resource on where to find the best lobster, how to eat it, and the story behind these tasty crustaceans.

the story of the lobster

IF YOU HAD ONE DOLLAR for each image of a lobster you saw on your travels around Mount Desert, you would leave a millionaire. They are everywhere: on signs, menus, advertisements, t-shirts, and, until recently, even on the Maine license plate. And (arguably) with good reason. Lobster fishing is one of the most important industries in the state of Maine, providing nearly half of all economic revenue from fishing. Each year Maine lobstermen haul in upwards of 20 million pounds of the tasty crustacean, 75% of the nation's total, to be served as a delicacy around the globe.

Since early colonial times lobsters have been a part of the New England diet. A simple and reliable source of food, they were plentiful in nearly every coastal bay. Since they were not frequently harvested, some were said to have reached sizes of up to five feet in length. In the early nineteenth century the area around Cape Cod was the major supplier of lobsters, but overfishing quickly depleted populations and fisherman then turned to the bountiful waters along the coast of Maine.

Soon lobster populations were depleted in Maine as well, and beginning in 1872 Maine enacted a series of laws aimed at conserving its natural resource. These laws made it illegal for lobstermen to take females bearing eggs or any lobster measuring over 10.5 inches in length. The measures were so successful that to the present day the annual lobster catch has proven remarkably steady.

Today the rules guiding lobster fishing state that all lobsters taken must be between 3 3/16 and 5 inches on the carapace - the area on the lobster from the eye socket to the back. These guidelines allow young lobsters to fully mature and large lobsters to continue breeding. Not only are egg-bearing females illegal to take, but lobstermen may even choose to cut a notch in their tails protecting them from ever being harvested by another lobstermen. Such is the tradeoff for bearing up to fifty thousand eggs per mating cycle. These guidelines ensure healthy lobster populations and are adhered to religiously by Maine lobstermen. In fact, the rules are taken so seriously that a lobsterman found violating them will often find his traps and buoys vandalized by other lobstermen.

Mature lobsters are found in depths ranging from 6 to 1,200 feet, with the greatest concentrations found in depths less than 180 feet. They tend to live along the rocky bottom in areas where kelp is plentiful. Lobsters are known to eat a variety of fish, mollusks, starfish, and sea urchins although they also have the ability to filter plankton from the water. Lobsters

The Distinguished Maine Lobster

Although today the Maine lobster is renowned as a sophisticated delicacy around the globe, its refined social status was not fully secured until relatively recently. Native Americans in the region avoided the lobster as a source of food and in the 1800s indentured servants required clauses in their contracts stating they would not have to be served lobster more than twice a week. Even the 1872 article in *Harper*'s that put Mount Desert Island on the map, noted, "The lobster business may be a profitable branch of industry, but [lobsters] are neither romantic nor poetical ... Just as [visitors to Mount Desert] are about to be ushered into this new world of romance and delight, [that they are] met upon the threshold by thousands of lobsters, raw, boiled, cooked, and canned, is discouraging to say the least." Luckily, Maine lobsters ignored such disparaging remarks and went on to become one of the most celebrated shellfish of all time.

smell food or bait using the antennae located at the front of the head and the tiny hairs on the legs. They are cannibalistic creatures that will attack smaller and injured lobsters when they can.

In order for a lobster to grow, it must periodically shed its skin in a process called molting. Just as a snake will shed its skin, so too will a lobster shed its shell. Before shedding its old shell, the lobster develops a new, paper-thin shell under its old one. After crawling out of its old shell, the lobster's new shell has the approximate consistency of a slab of Jell-O. During this stage the lobster is virtually defenseless and must find a hiding spot from predators until its new shell hardens. Each time a lobster molts, it increases its size by roughly 20 percent.

Unlike most macroscopic organisms, lobsters are asymmetrical - one lobster claw is always larger than the other. The larger claw is referred to as the "crusher claw" and is used to crush the shells of smaller crustaceans while the "ripper claw" is used to tear food apart. With names like crusher and ripper, you can understand why lobster claws are rubber-banded shut.

cowboys of the sea

ALMOST EVERY HARBOR on the coast of Maine has at least a dozen lobster boats that fish throughout the year. Each boat is between thirty and forty feet long and is manned by lobstermen working alone or in pairs. Often rising before dawn, lobstermen head directly to the docks where their boats are moored. If the weather is clear, they will row out to their boats and begin their long and physically demanding day. If the skies are overcast or the fog is thick, they will spend time at the dock talking with fellow lobstermen.

Lobster traps are usually located within ten miles of the shore. Underwater traps are connected by a line - called a warp - to floating Styrofoam buoys, each painted with the unique color coding of the lobsterman it belongs to. When a lobstermen reaches one of his buoys, he pulls it into the boat with a gaff and the warp is connected to the wheel of a hydraulic trap hauler. As the trap is hauled in, seawater and slime are sprayed about the cockpit. Once the trap is onboard, the lobsters are removed, their claws are immobilized, and they are placed in crates or barrels filled with seawater. The trap is then rebaited with a small bag full of herring, alewives, or menhaden. Any lobsters measuring under or over the legal limit are tossed back into the sea.

In American folklore, the Maine lobster fisherman often appears as the last of the rugged individualists. He is his own boss and his own man, willing to defend his independence with violence if necessary. His daily activities are dictated by weather and the turn of the seasons rather than by the office clock, governmental bureaucracy, or society's expectations. Fishermen tend to present themselves to tourists as men who earn their living from a relentless and icy sea with nothing but their skill, courage, and tenacity. If sophisticated urbanites chuckle at the rustics on the Maine docks, they do so with a tinge of envy, for the lobster fishermen embodies many of our most cherished virtues. He is, along with the farmer and rancher, the quintessential American.

-James M. Acheson, *The Lobster Gangs of Maine*

Lobstermen can pull between 150 and 500 traps a day, going through the same routine day in and day out. Trap locations are moved several times a year to compensate for the seasonal migration of lobster into warmer water. During peak season most lobstermen work from dawn till dusk, traveling from trap to trap with hardly a break. Arriving home after an exhausting day on the water, they catch the local weather report for the next day before turning in to bed.

In his book, *The Lobster Gangs of Maine*, James M. Acheson explains that the fishing grounds of lobstermen are often defined by the geographical boundaries of the harbor where they are based. Lobstermen from each harbor form social cliques or "gangs" as Acheson describes them, constantly interacting with one another but seldom coming into any contact with lobstermen from other harbors. Although no laws exist governing trap placement, the fishing boundaries between neighboring lobster gangs are often defined by history and staunchly defended at all costs. If a rival gang or even a single lobstermen attempts to encroach upon these boundaries, retaliation in the form of vandalized traps and buoys can be expected. In certain rare cases, full out "lobster wars " have occurred involving the widespread destruction of traps, equipment, and lobster boats.

Finding the Tastiest Lobster in Town

So you want the ultimate lobster dinner? Here's what you need to know. As any purist will tell you, the quintessential lobster dinner consists of one lobster boiled for 12 to 15 minutes with plenty of melted butter on the side for dipping and side dishes of corn, coleslaw, and potatoes. Although this seems like a recipe that even the lobster could perform, there are several factors influencing the flavor of your lobster that should be taken into consideration.

Lobsters must be kept alive up to the moment before they are cooked. Dead lobsters quickly develop toxins that can lead to severe sickness and, in rare cases, death. That's why lobsters are always kept in salt water tanks in restaurants and grocery stores. However, some restaurants simply keep a tank of live lobsters on display and serve customers meat that has been kept frozen until it is ready to be served. Restaurants that do serve lobsters taken directly from a saltwater tank can sometimes leave the same stagnant water in the tank for several months before changing it. Both of these scenarios might negatively influence the flavor of your lobster.

One rule of thumb to follow when selecting a lobster restaurant is to choose one as close to the water as possible. The closer a restaurant is to the ocean, the easier it is for them to frequently refresh the saltwater in their lobster tanks. Although this proximity does not ensure that the restaurant in question will properly care for their lobsters, chances are greater that they will. When in doubt, ask.

Also realize that lobster prices vary throughout the year. Lobsters molt in large numbers in the early summer and spend most of their time hiding from predators rather than climbing into lobster traps. This lack of supply drives their market price up, a problem that is further compounded by the influx of millions of tourists. As the summer progresses, although more hungry tourists pour into Maine, more lobsters have become active and wander into traps - an interesting parallel if you think about it. After Labor Day, demand for lobster plummets while the supply remains extremely high. Thus, fall is when lobster prices reach their annual lows. This is good to know if you are buying lobster at a fish market or other food store, but lobster prices in restaurants tend to remain fairly static throughout the year, regardless of the market price.

Finally, if you are looking for the true, platonic conception of the ultimate Maine Lobster Dining Experience, you must get thee to a lobster pound. These fine dining establishments usually consist of a simple shack on or near a pier where lobster is served on a paper plate and melted butter comes in a Styrofoam cup. Pretty it ain't, but that's exactly the point. You are there for the freshest, tastiest, most succulent lobster in the world; and that's exactly what you'll get. On Mount Desert, Beal's Lobster Pound in Southwest Harbor is the hands down favorite, with Thurston's in Bernard running a close second. At both restaurants you hand pick the lobster you want from a tank built into the ordering counter. You can even watch as fellow diners arrive by boat and tie up at the pier. This is true lobster dining as God intended it.

A Genuine Downeast Lobster Bake

1. Build a big fire near the shore

2. Toss enough rocks in the fire to create a small shelf. When the rocks have had a chance to heat up (about 20 mins), cover them with a few pounds of seaweed.

3. Place your fresh Maine lobsters on the seaweed and put freshly shucked ears of corn between them. If you want, place clams and mussels on top of the lobsters. Cover with another layer of seaweed.

4. Pour a healthy dose of saltwater over the seaweed and kick back.

5. After about forty minutes remove your meal. Make sure you have plenty of melted butter for dipping.

6. Exclaim, "Ayuh. That there's a right good suppah."

Note: If fire, rocks, and seaweed are not within easy reach, you can always cook your lobsters in a pot of boiling water. Boil hard-shell lobsters 10-12 minutes; Soft-shell 7-9 minutes.

Some people find placing lobsters in a pot of boiling water or on a shelf of steaming seaweed to be cruel and unusual crustacean punishment. PETA has been known to protest the annual Rockland lobster festival by dressing up in lobster costumes and screaming as they pretend to be boiled. If you would like to spare your lobster some pain, take a toothpick or other sharp object and plunge it deep into the lobster's eye socket. This pierces the lobster's brain and kills it instantly. Yes it's a little gross, but you are in fact saving the lobster a great deal of suffering later on.

How to Eat a Lobster

There's no way around it. Eating lobster is a messy affair. But follow these simple steps, and you can wash off that salty lobster juice with the pride of a job well done.

1. Twist off the claws

2. Crack open the claws with a metal cracker. Remove the meat.

3. Twist off the tail from the body. Remove the flippers.

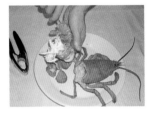

4. Insert a fork in the tail where the flippers used to be and push out the tail meat in one piece. Remove the black vein that runs the length of the tail.

5. Pull the shell of the body away from the underside. Discard the green substance found within. That's the liver, referred to as "tomalley."

6. Crack apart the underside in the middle. There are four pockets of meat found where the small legs are attached. You can also bite down on the legs with your teeth and suck out the meat inside.

restaurants

Island Restaurants Revealed

This dining guide does not represent a complete list of restaurants on the island. It is also not a list of the most expensive restaurants but rather a sampling of restaurants that, for one reason or another, have distinguished themselves and deserve special attention. The prices listed have been quoted as accurately as possible.

Dining room at the Bar Harbor Inn

Abel's Lobster Pound

Northeast Harbor

Abel's offers outdoor or indoor dining overlooking the northern part of Somes Sound. As lobster pounds go, this is towards the high end - and the only one on the island that offers sit down service.

Off Route 198
Entrees: $15 - 40
Reservations: suggested in Jul &Aug
Open Memorial - Columbus Day
Noon - 10pm, after Labor Day 5-9pm
276-5827

Anthony's Restaurant

Bar Harbor

Classic Italian food. Seafood features prominently on the menu and they do it well. Their seafood pesto lasagna, lobster asiago, and lobster fra diavolo are all recommended.

191 Main St.
Entrees: $9 - 25
Reservations: suggested
Open year round, 11am - 10pm, 9pm offseason
288-3377

Asticou Inn

Northeast Harbor

Their elegant dining room overlooks the head of Northeast Harbor. Food is top notch and the staff features cooks from the New England Culinary Institute. Sunday brunch is a Northeast Harbor tradition. Jacket & tie dinner attire.

Route 3
Entrees: $19 - 28
Reservations: suggested
Open mid -May - October
Breakfast: 7:30-9:30am Dinner: 6-9:30pm
276-3344

Bar Harbor Inn

Bar Harbor

The Bar Harbor Inn's Reading Room restaurant commands amazing views of Frenchman's Bay. The Reading Room offers upscale regional cuisine. Lunch and Sunday Brunch are offered on their oceanside terrace.

Newport Drive, next to the town pier
Entrees: $17 -30
Reservations: recommended
Open April - November, 11:30am - 9:30pm
288-3351

Beal's Lobster Pound

Southwest Harbor

A genuine lobster pound located right on the water. You hand pick the lobster you want from a tank built into the ordering counter. As you enjoy your meal, you can watch fellow diners arrive via boat and tie up on the pier. Lobster dining as God intended it.

Clark Point Road
Entrees: Seafood prices vary
Reservations: no
Open mid-May - Mid-Oct, 9am -8pm
244-3202

Burning Tree

Otter Creek (South of Bar Harbor)

Best gourmet seafood. The coast of Maine is one of the few places cold enough to harvest giant scallops, and the Burning Tree offers them on their menu. Edible flowers garnish the dishes red meat is conspicuously absent from the menu.

Route 3
Entrees: $15 - 20
Reservations: recommended
Open for dinner, late June - Oct, Wed - Mon
288-9331

The Bistro at Seal Harbor

Seal Harbor

One of the best kept gourmet secrets. With only a half-dozen tables, getting a reservation here can be a bit of a challenge. As for the atmosphere, as one Seal Harbor resident so aptly described it, "People come down from the hill [Ox Hill where Martha Stewart owns an estate] to eat there."

Main Street
Entrees:$16 - 23
Reservations: required
Open June - mid-Oct, Tues - Sun 6-10pm
276-3299

Cafe Bluefish

Bar Harbor

Fantastic upscale dining. Cafe Bluefish's nondescript location is often overlooked by visitors, but not by the nine national publications that have handed them top notch reviews. Their dinner strudels are some of the tastiest things you will ever put in your mouth.

122 Cottage St.
Entrees: $15 - 22
Reservations: recommended
Open May - Oct, 5:30 - close
288-3696

Claremont Hotel

Southwest Harbor

Breakfast and dinner are offered from the upscale Claremont Hotel's dining room, which offers spectacular views of Somes Sound. Lunch and cocktails are also offered from their waterfront boathouse. Jacket required for dinner, credit cards not accepted.

Claremont Hotel, off Main Street
Entrees: $19 - 23
Reservations: required
Open 8 - 10am, 12 - 2pm, 5 - 9pm
244-5036

Eat-A-Pita / Chef Marc

Southwest Harbor

The most remarkable aspect of this place is its nightly Clark Kent-like transformation from a mild mannered pita shop into one of the best restaurants on the island. During the day you can get healthy and delicious pita sandwiches. At night Chef Marc serves gourmet food at surprisingly reasonable prices. Breakfast is also available.

326 Main St.
Entrees: $11 - 24
Reservations: no
Open mid-May - late-Oct, 8am - 10pm
244-4344

Elaine's Starlight Oasis

Bar Harbor

Vegetarian cuisine. Quietly tucked away on West Street, most people don't even realize it's there, but Elaine's offers great dining in a cozy atmosphere. Tofu and vegan dishes feature prominently on the menu, but the food is quite filling.

78 West St.
Entrees: $10 - 13
Reservations: recommended
Open 5pm - close, closed Mon
288-3287

EPI Sub & Pizza

Bar Harbor

Generally considered to have the best subs on the island. Fast, cheap, and good. A great place to get take out food for hiking or a picnic lunch.

8 Cottage St.
Entrees: $4 - 14
Reservations: no
Open Feb - Dec, 10am - 9pm
288-5853

Fiddler's Green   Southwest Harbor

Gourmet dining. Seared duck breast with a pomegranate glaze, mussels steamed in Guinness Stout! There's a reason this is one of the best restaurants on the island. Their dining room also overlooks Southwest Harbor.

411 Main St.
Entrees: $17 - 24
Reservations: recommended
Open May - mid Dec, 5:30 - 9:30pm
244-9416

Fish House Grill   Bar Harbor

Standard dinner fare with a seafood emphasis. The real attraction here is the waterfront dining right next to the Town Pier. They offer both indoor and outdoor seating, if possible request a table outside.

1 West Street
Entrees: $12 - 22
Reservations: no
Open May - Oct, 11:30am - Midnight

Freddie's Route 66   Bar Harbor

Bar Harbor's version of the Hard Rock Cafe, but here the theme is 50s memorabilia. Family dining where the emphasis is on the atmosphere.

21 Cottage St
Entrees: $9 - 20
Reservations: no
Open May - Oct, 11:30am - Midnight
288-3708

Full Belli Deli   Northeast Harbor

An extensive menu of gourmet sandwiches. Their speciality is caramelized onion relish - a sticky, sweet concoction that can transform any sandwich into desert. Best lunch spot in the vicinity of Northeast Harbor.

Sea Street
Entrees: $4 - 6
Reservations: no
Open Mon - Sat, 7am - 2pm
276-4299

George's   Bar Harbor

Located in a restored summer cottage, George's features upscale, Mediterranean based cuisine. Specialities include wild game, lamb, and seafood. Extensive wine list.

7 Stephen's Lane
Entrees: $25
Reservations: recommended
Open mid-June - Oct, 5:30pm - close
288-4505

Havana   Bar Harbor

American fine dining with a Latin flair. Havana burst onto the scene in 1999 and promptly became an instant classic. The menu changes weekly. One of the most high profile restaurants on the island.

7 Stephen's Lane
Entrees: $15 - 25
Reservations: recommended
Open Mar - Jan, 6 - 10pm
288-2822

Island Chowder House   Bar Harbor

Chowder is their specialty. Award winning chowder to be exact. They also serve seafood, steaks, and other standard fare. And don't miss the model train that circles the dining room.

38 Cottage St.
Entrees: $8 - 17
Reservations: no
Open mid-May - Oct, 11am - 10pm
288-4905

Islesford's Dock Restaurant   Islesford (Little Cranberry Island)

Overlooking the water next to the town pier, their dining room commands a stunning view of the mountains of Mount Desert. Water taxi service back to Northeast Harbor is available after dinner. Fresh seafood is the emphasis.

Islesford Town Pier
Entrees: $8 - 25
Reservations: suggested for dinner
Open mid-June - Oct, 11am - 3pm, 5 - 9pm
244-7494

Jordan's Restaurant   Bar Harbor

A popular early morning fueling spot.
Jordan's throws open their doors at five
A.M. and proceeds to cook up their classic
blueberry pancakes - code name, "order of
blues." Nothing fancy, just good, filling
breakfast food.

80 Cottage St.
Entrees: $3 - 7
Reservations: no
Open late March - mid-Feb, 5am - 2pm
288-3586

Jordan Pond House   Seal Harbor

I've said it before and I'll say it again:
Popovers at the Jordan Pond House
should be required by law. Although most
people pop in for this quick snack (get it?),
they offer a full lunch and dinner menu too.
Million-dollar views are offered at a fraction
of the price.

Park Loop Road
Entrees: $9 - 18
Reservations: no, but preferred seating
Open mid-May - late Oct
11:30am - 8pm, 9pm in July and Aug
276-3316

Little Notch Cafe   Southwest Harbor

A great lunch spot in Southwest Harbor.
Focaccia bread sandwiches and creative
pizzas plus homemade soups and chow-
ders.

340 Main St.
Entrees: $3 - 12
Reservations: no
Open year round, Mon - Sat, 11am - 8pm
244-3357

Lompoc Cafe & Brewpub   Bar Harbor

The Lompoc Cafe & Brewpub specializes
in middle eastern and mediterranean cuisine like hummus, stuffed grape leaves,
and vegetarian and seafood entrees. They
also offer open air seating next to their own
private boccie garden.

36 Rodick St.
Entrees: $8 - 15
Reservations: no
Open mid-May - mid Oct, 11:30am - 1am
288-9392

Maggie's Classic Scales

Bar Harbor

Quietly hidden off of Cottage Street, Maggie's offers gourmet dining with a diligent emphasis on using only the freshest ingredients. They buy their fish off the Bar Harbor Pier and use locally grown organic vegetables, many from their own garden.

6 Summer St., off of Bridge St.
Entrees: $14 - 21
Reservations: recommended
Open mid-June - mid Oct, 5 - 9:30pm
288-9007

Mama Dimatteo's

Bar Harbor

Regional American cuisine with an Italian emphasis. Vegetarian and seafood selections feature prominently on the menu, but they also offer red meat favorites like tenderloin and ribs.

34 Kennebec Place, NW of Village Green
Entrees: $11 - 19
Reservations: recommended
Open year round, 5pm to close
288-3666

Michelle's

Bar Harbor

"French-American cuisine with a New England flair." They've been honored with the AAA four diamond award. Despite the pricey menu, the attire is casual, and you can dine outside or in one of their decadent indoor dining rooms.

194 Main St
Entrees: $20 - 64
Reservations: preferred
Open May - Oct, 6 - 10pm
288-0038

Miguel's

Bar Harbor

Mexican restaurant serving enchiladas, fajitas, and other standard fare. More sophisticated choices include Blue Corn Crab Cakes and Marinated Snapper.

51 Rodick St.
Entrees: $4 - 15
Reservations: for parties of 10 or more
Open mid-March - Oct, 5pm - close
288-5117

Mooring's   Manset

Mooring's offers slightly upscale seafood and steak fare, but the real attraction here is their sweeping, breathtaking, unbeliev-able, amazing view of Somes Sound. If you're looking for inexpensive food in a great setting, this is your place.

Shore Road, across from Hinckley Store
Entrees: $9 - 15
Reservations:no
Open mid-March - Oct, 5pm - close
244-7070

Nakorn Thai   Bar Harbor

This is the best Asian food on the island. It is also the only Asian food on the island. Still, if you feel like something different it's worth checking out. The menu consists of your usual Thai specialties, Pad Thai, Kom Kar Gar, etc.

30 Rodick St.
Entrees: $7 - 13
Reservations: no
Open April - Oct, 11am - 10pm, wkend 4 - 10pm
288-4060

Olde Flame BBQ Pit   Bar Harbor

Genuine BBQ? In Maine? I've had several friends from Texas tell me the Olde Flame is on par with the best BBQ to be had in the Lone Star State. These guys bring out 6 dif-ferent BBQ sauces with each meal, and all meats are smoked on the premises.

131 Cottage St.
Entrees: $9 - 20
Reservations: no
Open mid-March - Jan, 11:30am - 1am
288-2800

124 Cottage St   Bar Harbor

Extensive menu of a wide range of upscale food. They also feature a 45-item salad bar that is offered as an entree for $10.

124 Cottage St.
Entrees: $12 - 23
Reservations: recommended
Open June - Oct, 5 - 10pm
288-4383

Pier Restaurant
Bar Harbor

Located right on the water overlooking the Bar Harbor and the Porcupine Islands. They offer deli sandwiches, but the emphasis here is on fresh, delicious seafood. Indoor and outdoor seating.

55 West St.
Entrees: $5 - 19
Reservations: no
Open 7am - 9:30pm, daily
288-2110

Preble Grill
Southwest Harbor

Regional cuisine with a Mediterranean influence. The Preble Grill was a *Yankee* Magazine Editor's Pick for their gourmet food and great deserts.

14 Clark Point Road
Entrees: $9 - 25
Reservations: recommended
Open 5 - 10pm daily
244-3034

Redfield's
Northeast Harbor

Gourmet dining is offered at this ever popular Northeast Harbor restaurant. Open in the late afternoon for cocktails and appetizers.

Main Street
Entrees: $15 - 22
Reservations: required
Open year round, closed Sundays
276-5283

Rosalie's Pizza
Bar Harbor

Hands down the best pizza on the island. In fact, Rosalie's is consistently ranked as one of the top three pizza places in Maine. You can get just about anything you want on your pizza, but if you like garlic and spinach try their Rosalie's Choice Pizza. Their stuffed slices also deserve gold medal marks.

46 Cottage St.
Entrees: $4 - 15
Reservations: no
Open April - November, 11:30am - 9:30pm
288-5666

Rose Garden Restaurant

Bar Harbor (at the Bluenose Inn)

Recipient of the five diamond award. Gourmet dining in one of the newest upscale hotels on the island.

Route 3, north of Bar Harbor
Entrees: $30, four course $52 prix fixe menu
Reservations: recommended
Open April - November, 5:30 - 9:30pm
288-3351

Rupununi

Bar Harbor

Reasonably priced upscale food makes this one of the most popular restaurants in Bar Harbor. Here you'll find seafood, sirloin, and a burger list that includes beef, turkey, ostrich, and buffalo burgers. They offer outdoor seating in the heart of Bar Harbor.

119 Main St.
Entrees: $8 - 19
Reservations: no
Open April - Oct, 11am - 1am
288-2886

Thurston's

Tremont

Much like Beal's in Southwest Harbor, Thurston's is a genuine lobster pound where the emphasis is on the lobster. Diners arriving by boat also tie up next to Thurston's Pier.

Steamboat Wharf Road
Entrees: $5 - 30
Reservations: no
Open Mem - Columbus Day, 11am - 8:30pm
244-7600

Two Cats

Bar Harbor

A great breakfast and lunch place. That's all they offer and they do it well. Breakfast ranges from standard to upscale, like their Mediterranean breakfast with sundried tomato polenta, eggs, feta, etc. Lunch offerings include gourmet soups and sandwiches.

130 Cottage St.
Lunches: $4 - 8
Reservations: no
Open 7am - 2pm daily
288-2808

Village Green

Bar Harbor

Bakery and cafe featuring an extensive breakfast menu and diner style lunches. Dinner is also available.

195 Main Street
Lunches: $4 - 15, dinner: $8 - 15
Reservations: no
Open Jan - Oct, 6:30am - 9pm daily
288-9450

XYZ Restaurant

Manset

I almost considered not making this list alphabetical so these guys wouldn't wind up last. This is a genuine Mexican restaurant where burritos, enchiladas, and chimichangas are not included on the menu. That hasn't stopped the *NY Times*, *Boston Globe*, or *Gourmet Getaways* from handing them top notch reviews.

Shore Road
Entrees: $15
Reservations: required
Open mid-May - mid-Oct, 5:30 - 9pm
244-5221

Bibliography

Acheson, James M. *The Lobster Gangs of Maine*. Hanover, NH: University Press of New England, 1988

Belanger, Pamela J. *Inventing Acadia, Artists and Tourists at Mount Desert*. Hanover, NH: University Press of New England, 1999

Brandes, Kathleen M. *Maine Handbook*. Chico, CA. Moon Publications, Inc. 1998

Collier, Sargent F. *Mount Desert Island & Acadia National Park, an Informal History* Camden, ME: Downeast Books, 1978

Coffin, Tammis E. *The Rusticator's Journal*. Bar Harbor, ME: Friends of Acadia, 1993

Elfring, Chris. *AMC Guide to Mount Desert Island and Acadia National Park* Boston, MA: Appalachian Mountain Club Books, 1993

Eliot, Charles W. *John Gilley, One of the Forgotten Millions*. Bar Harbor, ME: Acadia Press, 1989

Evans, Lisa Gollin. *An Outdoor Family Guide to Acadia National Park*. Seattle, WA: The Mountaineers, 1997

Fernald, Meg. *One Man's Museum, The Story of the Islesford Historical Museum*. Eastern National Park & Monument Association, 1990

Gilman, Richard A. *The Geology of Mount Desert Island*. Maine Geological Survey, Department of Conservation, 1988

Gillmore, Robert. *Great Walks of Acadia National Park and Mount Desert Island* Goffstown, NH: Great Walks Inc., 1994

Hanson, Gunnar. *Mount Desert, An Informal History*. Town of Mount Desert, ME: 1989

Helfich, G.W. & O'Neil, Gladys. *Lost Bar Harbor*. Camden, ME: Downeast Books, 1982

Lee, Donna Marie & Ivey, Jean Marie. *Facts and Fancy, Acadia*. Ellsworth, ME: Facts and Fancy Universal, 1993

Minutolo, Audrey, *Biking on Mount Desert Island*. Camden, ME: Downeast Books, 1996

Motorists Guide Park Loop Road. Eastern National: 1999

Newlin, William V.P. *Lakes & Ponds of Mt. Desert*. Camden, ME: Downeast Books, 1989

Roberts, Ann Rockefeller. *Mr. Rockefeller's Roads, The Untold Story of Acadia's Carriage Roads and Their Creator*. Camden, ME: Downeast Books, 1990

Rothe, Robert. *Acadia, The Story Behind the Scenery*. Las Vegas, NV: KC Publications, 1979

Thayer, Robert A. *The Park Loop Road, A Guide to Acadia National Park's Scenic Byway*. Camden, ME: Downeast Books, 1999

Sanger, David & Prins, Harald E.L. *An Island in Time*. Bar Harbor, ME: Robert Abbe Museum, 1989

Sharpe, Grant W. Ph.D. *A Guide to Acadia National Park*. New York: Golden Press, 1968

Spurling, Ted. *The Town of Cranberry Isles*. Brownsville, VT: 1979

St. Germain, *Trails of History, The Story of Mount Desert Island's Paths from Norumbega to Acadia* Bar Harbor, ME: Parkman Publications, 1993

Vandenbergh, Lydia & Shettleworth, Earle G., Jr. *Revisiting Seal Harbor and Acadia National Park*. Dover, NH: Arcadia Publishing, 1997

index

index